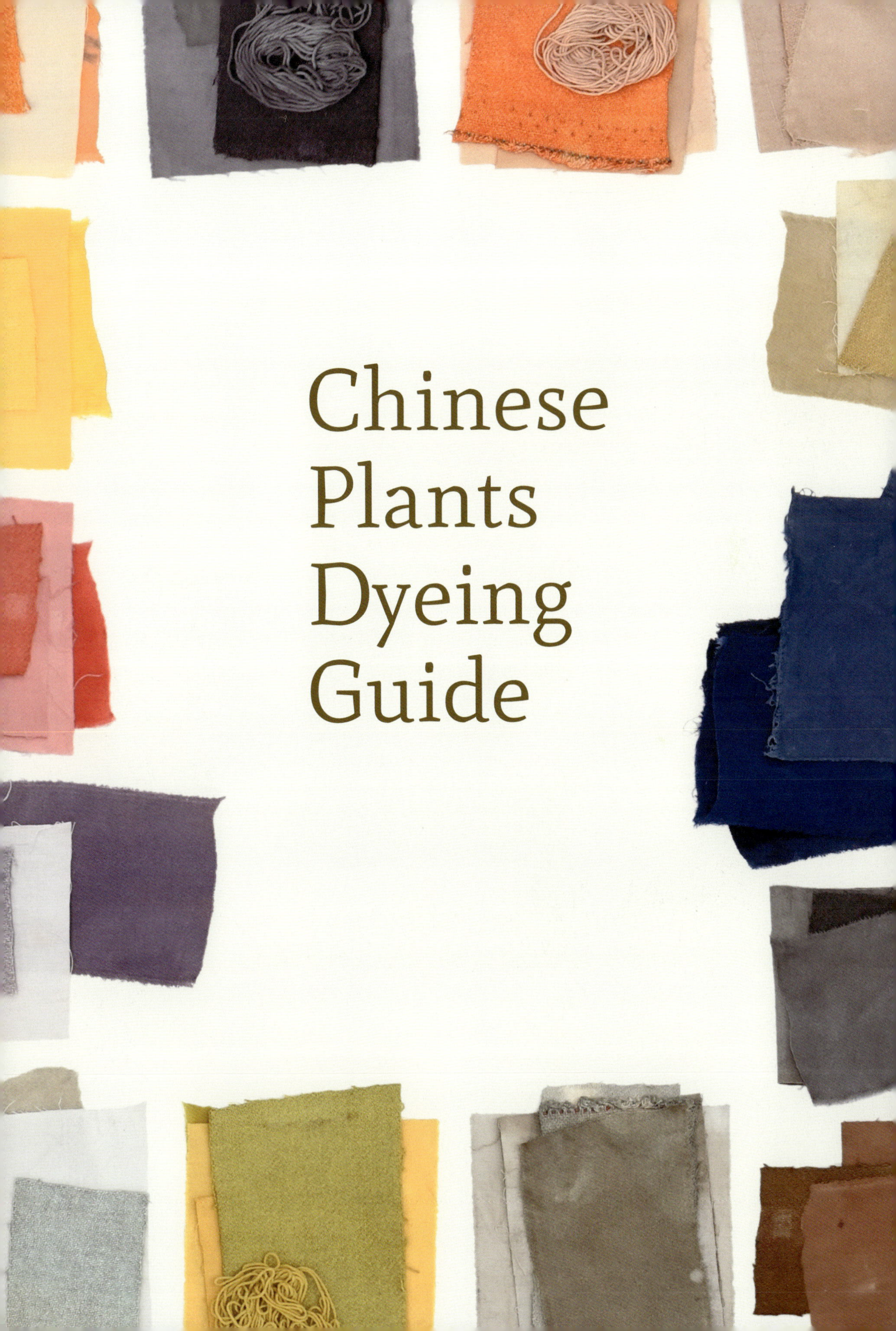

Chinese Plants Dyeing Guide

Chinese Plants Dyeing Guide
Techniques for Creating Natural Dye Projects at Home
By Zhou Jiao
SCPG

On pages 1–3
Plants used in this book and the dye samples produced from them.

Top
A selection of tie-dye pieces created by the author.

Text: Zhou Jiao
Photographs: Zhou Jiao, Zhou Feiyu

Translation: Shelly Bryant
Cover Design: Chen Ruiduo
Interior Design: Li Jing, Hu Bin (Yuan Yinchang Design Studio)

Editor: Qiu Yan

ISBN: 978-1-63288-045-1

Address any comments about *Chinese Plants Dyeing Guide* to:

SCPG
401 Broadway, Ste. 1000
New York, NY 10013
USA

or

Shanghai Press and Publishing Development Co., Ltd.
Floor 5, No. 390 Fuzhou Road, Shanghai, China (200001)
Email: sppd@sppdbook.com

Printed in China by RR Donnelley Asia Printing Solutions Limited

1 3 5 7 9 10 8 6 4 2

CONTENTS

CHAPTER ONE
Understanding Plant Dyeing

Plant dyeing is an ancient craft that has been passed down for thousands of years. It is the most natural and sustainable dyeing method, shaped by historical accumulation. It embodies the wisdom of human labor and life, showcasing the wonders and charm of nature. The plant dyes in this book are sourced from nature and used in harmony with it, extracting the essence of flowers, trees, and herbs to add rich colors to natural fabrics. Plant dyeing is not only a craft but also a culture, a tradition, and a profound interpretation of the beauty of nature. Let us step into the world of plant dyeing, explore the colorful stories accumulated over the years, and experience the perfect fusion of nature and culture.

1. The History of Traditional Chinese Plant Dyeing

China's dyeing techniques have a long, rich history. People extracted dyes from minerals, plants, and animals to engage in dyeing activities, dating back as early as the Late Paleolithic period.

Ornaments coated with hematite powder were discovered in the cave at the Peking Man Site in Zhoukoudian, Beijing. This is the earliest known example of mineral dyeing ever found. The dyeing methods at that time were relatively simple: minerals were crushed, mixed with water, and then applied to fabrics. Early minerals used for dyeing included hematite, cinnabar, realgar, azurite, and lead white. Later, with the rise and development of plant-based dyeing, plant dyes gradually surpassed mineral dyes in terms of dye extraction and refinement, the richness of color spectrums, colorfastness, and economic value. As a result, mineral dyes were gradually replaced by plant dyes.

Although mineral dyes are still in use today, they are primarily applied in paper-based painting. Compared to mineral dyes, plant-based dyes offer a much wider variety of materials, with hundreds of plant species used for

On the facing page
Dye samples from betel nut using different mordants.

dyeing throughout history. The range of colors that can be achieved is far more diverse, and the process is also more environmentally friendly.

China is one of the earliest countries to use plant-based dyes. According to research, there are currently four main types of origins for plant dyeing practices:

1. The primitive, direct discovery. In ancient times, humans painted plant juices onto their bodies for entertainment or ritual activities. Over time, they gradually realized that certain plants had dyeing properties and began applying them to fabrics, using direct application methods to add color.

2. During the process of preparing food, people discovered that certain plants easily imparted color, such as red cabbage and gardenia fruits used as a seasoning in chicken soup.

3. It was found during the preparation of traditional Chinese medicine that many medicinal plants not only released their therapeutic properties when decocted but also extracted pigments, with the extraction process being highly similar to the preparation of dye liquids.

4. Discoveries were made during the blending of fragrances. For example, in the process of brewing wine, various plants were often added to enhance the aroma and harmonize colors. These plants, after being soaked for extended periods, would release their water soluble pigments more easily, making it possible to later apply the extracted pigments to the field of dyeing.

Documentation related to plant-based dyeing is abundant and detailed, and such techniques are still widely used today. In contrast, records and applications of animal derived dyes are relatively scarce. Examples include dyes from murex shells and purple dye mollusks. Since few animals are capable of producing dye, and because of their strong geographic limitations, rarity of species, and the difficulty of obtaining them, animal dyes were neither widely adopted nor extensively documented.

China had already been extensively using plant-based dyes as early as the Shang (1600–1046 BC) and Zhou (1046–256 BC) dynasties. The practice saw tremendous development during the Han (202 BC–220 AD) and Tang (618–907) dynasties and reached a high level of maturity and specialization by the Ming (1368–1644) and Qing (1644–1911) periods. Both the range of dye plants and color spectrums, as well as dyeing and printing techniques, continued to be refined over time. This chapter provides readers with an overview of the history of traditional Chinese plant dyeing, covering four aspects, dyeing institutions, dye plants and their colors, dyeing methods, and printing and dyeing techniques.

Establishment of Dyeing Institutions

In every dynasty of China, there were dedicated dyeing institutions and officials appointed specifically to oversee dyeing affairs, ensuring the production of dyed materials for imperial use. Starting from the Zhou

An illustration from the *Textile Album*, painted by Wu Qi during the Qing dynasty.

dynasty, there have been documented historical records detailing dyeing practices and related matters. During the Western Zhou period (1046–771 BC), there were positions called Dyeing Personnel and Dyeing Materials Supervisor, each responsible for different dyeing tasks. The Dyeing Personnel were primarily in charge of the actual dyeing process, while the Dyeing Materials Supervisor was responsible for collecting the dyeing materials. During the Qin dynasty (221–206 BC), there was an institution called the Dyeing Division. From the Han dynasty to the Sui dynasty (581–618), there was a Dyeing Bureau. During the Tang and Song (960–1279) dynasties, there was a Dyeing Institute, and in the Ming and Qing dynasties, there was a Dyeing Office.

Some images depicting textile production techniques have been preserved to this day, such as the *Textile Album* painted by the Qing dynasty artist Wu Qi (1642–1718). The album consists of 20 pages, created with color on silk, and intricately depicts processes such as silkworm moths, reeling silk, spinning silk, weaving, and garment making. Reeling silk refers to the process of turning silkworm cocoons into raw silk by boiling, pulling, and winding the threads, which separates the silk from the cocoon and forms continuous silk threads. Spinning silk refers to the further processing of the raw silk after reeling, winding it into a suitable form for weaving or dyeing, which is a post-processing step for raw silk.

The image above is one of these illustrations, depicting a dyeing workshop scene where five men, from left to right, are stirring dye vats, twisting silk threads, transporting dye, hanging dye on shoulders to dry, and immersing silk threads into the dye. In the center of the scene, there is a tool used for stacking fabric. In the foreground, un-dyed silk threads are being dried, while dyed red silk threads are hanging in a shaded area beneath the eaves. From the busy activity depicted in the image, it is clear that the dyeing process was highly specialized and well organized.

With the changing of dynasties, the dyeing institutions and official positions evolved from initially simple divisions between dyeing operations and dye material collection into specialized dyeing workshops with very detailed roles. The *Six Statutes of the Tang Dynasty* records that during the Tang dynasty, there were six different dyeing workshops specifically dedicated to blue (青), red (绛), yellow, white, black-gray (皂), and purple dyes.

Different regions also specialized in dyeing specific colors derived from plants. During the Qing dynasty, the Jiangsu and Zhejiang (in East China) regions were known for their expertise in dyeing blue and green hues. This specialization was further divided among various cities, such as Nanjing (capital city of Jiangsu Province), which excelled in dyeing sky blue and indigo; Suzhou (a city in Jiangsu Province), known for its expertise in sky blue, royal blue, second blue, and onion blue; and Hangzhou (capital city of Zhejiang Province), which specialized in lake color, light blue, snow blue, jade color, and dark green.

The evolution of dyeing institutions' functions reveals that over time, the number of colors that could be achieved through dyeing increased, and the classifications became more detailed. This indicates that the dyeing techniques became increasingly systematic and refined.

The Development of Dyeing Plants and Colors

To study the history of plant dyeing, one must first look for dye related content in historical literature, and secondly, examine textile archaeological artifacts. This includes analyzing the fabric's age, color, pigment composition, patterns, and other aspects. Compared to artifacts such as ceramics and metals, textiles are more prone to deterioration due to centuries of burial, making textile archaeology more difficult and limiting the historical periods that can be inferred. In humid regions like the Central Plains, the color of textiles is even harder to preserve due to moisture, and the older the fabric, the darker its color tends to be.

According to historical records, during the Shang and Zhou dynasties, around ten commonly used dye plants were documented. These included indigo plants for blue dyeing, madder and knotweed for red, purple gromwell for purple, creek grass, foxglove, and smoke tree for yellow, and acorn for black.

The image on the right shows a textile fragment from the Western Zhou period, unearthed in Qiemo County, Xinjiang Uygur Autonomous Region

A textile fragment from the Western Zhou period, unearthed in Xinjiang, China.

(in Northwest China), and currently housed in the Xinjiang Museum. The textile is woven with yellow, red, and blue wool, demonstrating the diversity of plant dye colors and the variety of materials used in dyed textiles at that time.

During the Han and Tang dynasties, the number of dye plants expanded to nearly 30 species. These included madder, safflower, sappanwood, birch leaved pear, knotweed, and holly for red dyes; creek grass, gardenia fruit, foxglove, barberry, goldenrain tree, amur cork tree, smoke tree, and silkworm thorn tree for yellow; indigo plants like Chinese indigo, Chinese rain bell, true indigo, and woad for dyeing blue; purple gromwell and Indian spinach for purple; and sawtooth oak, Chinese tallow, three lobe beggar ticks, and Chinese chaste tree for black.

Textiles excavated from the Mawangdui Han tomb in Changsha, Hunan Province (in Central China), contained more than 20 colors, including red, orange, yellow, green, purple, brown, and black. In the Eastern Han dynasty (25–220), the *Shuowen Jiezi*, a Chinese dictionary, listed 39 different color names for textiles. During the Ming and Qing dynasties, the number of plants available for dyeing greatly increased. In the Ming dynasty, the *Tianshui Bingshan Lu*, a list of the property of an official of the time, recorded 44 color names for textiles. By the end of the Qing dynasty, the *Principles and Stitchings of Chinese Embroidery* recorded that textile colors could be divided into seven major categories—blue, red, yellow, green, purple, white, and vermilion—totaling 88 colors. If the colors were further classified by lightness and darkness, the range of colors would be even more complex.

With the development of plant dyeing, many common people made a living by specifically cultivating dye plants, and the number of artisans engaged in dyeing work also increased. According to the *Ming Wanli Shilu* (*Veritable Records of the Ming Dynasty*), there were thousands of dyeing artisans in Suzhou alone. At the same time, East-West trade also facilitated the development of dyeing techniques. China exported a large number of plants, such as safflower, madder, purple gromwell, and Chinese nutgall, to Europe, India, Japan, and other regions. Additionally, some foreign plants were introduced to China, such as woad, which was brought from Europe. Moreover, safflower was initially introduced to China by Zhang Qian from the Western Regions, and later it was widely cultivated within the country and exported.

For the standardization of plant dye color palettes, the ancient Chinese had a very romantic approach. Although in ancient times, there was no precise analysis of color wavelengths or lab values, the ancient people had a remarkably high sensitivity to color. Each color had its own specific name, and the ancient Chinese would often add descriptive words to evoke associations, helping to convey the nuances or inclinations of a particular color within a color family. For example, the depiction of different shades of red includes terms like crimson red (绛红), silver red (银红), water red (水红), and orangutan red (猩红). Yellow shades include goose yellow (鹅黄), orange yellow (橘黄), apricot yellow (杏黄), golden yellow (金黄), and earth yellow (土黄). Blues include egg blue (蛋青), sky blue (天青), vermilion blue (赤青), and dark blue (藏青). Greens include lake green (湖绿), bean green (豆绿), leaf green (叶绿), and fruit green (果绿). To ensure consistency and precision in color comparison, the feathers of birds were used as color standards, a practice recorded in both the *Rites of Zhou* and the *Book of the Later Han, Chapter on Carriages and Clothing*. Looking back, this was indeed a brilliant measure, indicating that standardized procedures for dyeing had already been developed at that time.

Plant dyeing also laid the foundation for the concept of the Five Elements and Five Colors in Chinese color theory. The Five Elements and Five Colors system represents a unique combination of ancient Chinese philosophy and color theory. Beginning with the Zhou dynasty, the Five Elements, Wood, Fire, Earth, Metal, Water, were associated with the five pure colors cyan (青), vermilion (赤), yellow (黄), white (白), and black (黑). In the *Rites of Zhou*, the chapter *Records of Craftsmen* combined the Five Colors with directions, Cyan East, Vermilion South, Yellow Center, White West, Black North, establishing a hierarchical system where "pure colors" were considered superior and "intermediate colors" inferior, alongside the ceremonial rule "wear pure colors on robes, and intermediate colors on skirts." The "pure colors" (cyan, vermilion, yellow, white, black) symbolized power and were used in the attire of emperors and ceremonial objects. The colors obtained by mixing the five standard colors are called intermediate colors, which include green (绿), red (红), turquoise (碧), purple (紫),

and sulfur yellow (硫黄), and were used by commoners.

This system was practically implemented through plant dyeing techniques, such as indigo plants for dyeing cyan, madder for vermilion, gardenia for yellow, and acorn for black. These colors were closely tied to political symbols. The reddish yellow dye was monopolized by the royal family, indigo blue became widespread among the common people, and black was used in official robes to signify authority. However, as dyeing technology developed and an increasing variety of new colors were produced, the possibilities for color selection grew dramatically. Coupled with the rulers' preferences for certain colors, the five elements and five colors system gradually became unable to meet the new demands and eventually began to break down.

The history of traditional Chinese plant dyeing began during the Shang and Zhou dynasties. The number of dyeing plants expanded from a dozen to dozens, and the color spectrum evolved from a single tone to a complex array. Basic color families such as red, yellow, and blue gave rise to more than a hundred symbolic hues, each reflecting the ancient people's wisdom in labor and their philosophy of aesthetics.

The Development of Dyeing Methods

Plant dyeing methods are mainly divided into three types, direct dyeing, over dyeing, and mordant dyeing. Direct dyeing involves soaking the material in a single dye solution, and it can be done once or multiple times. During the Warring States (475–221 BC) to Western Han (202 BC–AD 220) period, the text *Chapter of Utensils* in *Ready Guide* recorded, "One dyeing is called *quan* (reddish yellow), two dyeings is called *cheng* (deep red), and three dyeings is called *xun* (crimson)." This passage refers to the process of multiple immersions to achieve different shades of red. The first dyeing results in

Color samples dyed with safflower extract after different immersion times.

Fragments of colorful silk from the Han dynasty, unearthed in Dunhuang, Gansu Province, China.

a light red color similar to pink or orange or reddish yellow, the second dyeing turns it into a more vivid red, and the third dyeing yields a rich, deep red color. This indicates that people at the time had already mastered the technique of gradually deepening the color of fabric through multiple immersions. This method not only met the demand for different colors but also allowed for the creation of color variations and gradations by controlling the number of dyeing sessions. As shown in the image on page 13, the color changes that occur when using safflower for dyeing, from a single immersion to multiple immersions, are illustrated.

Over dyeing involves using two or more dyes applied sequentially to the fabric, resulting in a new mixed color. This technique was already in use during the Western Zhou period and had become quite refined by the Han dynasty. As shown in the image above, fragments of colorful silk from the Han dynasty, excavated from the Xuanquan site in Dunhuang, Gansu Province (in Northwest China), and now housed in the Gansu Bamboo and Silk Texts Museum, demonstrates this technique. The two pieces of green silk clearly show a yellow hue that emerges from the underlying layer. Both pieces of green fabric were first soaked in a yellow dye bath and then dyed blue to achieve the green color. The use of over dyeing greatly expanded the dye color spectrum. By applying over dyeing on top of varying levels of initial dye absorption, the resulting colors become even more rich and complex. As a result, the *Principles and Stitchings of Chinese Embroidery* recorded over 800 different colors of silk embroidery threads.

Mordant dyeing involves adding different mordants to cause a change in the color of a single dye bath, while also improving the colorfastness of the dye. Mordants are mainly divided into two categories, aluminum salts and iron salts. In ancient China, certain mineral salts containing metals were referred to as "alum." White alum and green alum were the earliest used mordants, and over time, other agents such as acid-base reagents and alcohol were developed as auxiliary substances.

As early as the Western Zhou period, there are records in the literature regarding the selection and usage methods of mordants, indicating that people had already distinguished between direct dyeing and mordant dyeing. By the Song dynasty, official institutions had been established to manage the mining and refining of alum. Research on mordanting was not only applied to dyeing but also to the precipitation of certain dye molecules. For example, after safflower was dyed, if a few drops of alkaline solution were added to the fabric, the safflower pigment could dissolve in water. This method was also used in situations where there was an urgent need to use safflower as a medicinal herb.

The methods of direct dyeing, over dyeing, and mordant dyeing developed in parallel with the emergence of plant dyeing. The ancients quickly mastered the key techniques of these methods, and as the number of dyeing plants increased, the new colors created through these methods became increasingly diverse.

The Development of Printing and Dyeing Techniques

Direct dyeing and mordant dyeing can create gradient or shading effects on fabric based on a single hue. However, to produce patterns or designs on fabric, printing and dyeing techniques are required. During the Qin and Han dynasties in China, resist dyeing techniques had already begun to emerge, allowing patterns to be created on fabrics by preventing dye from penetrating certain areas.

Techniques such as tie-dyeing and wax resistant dyeing (batik) were already in use at that time. As shown in the image on the right, these are fragments of a blue-ground patterned printed woolen fabric from the Northern Dynasties period (439–581), unearthed from the Astana tombs in Xinjiang. The image clearly shows water droplet-shaped petals created using the wax-resist dyeing technique. The petals are light yellow, and the background is a deep blue.

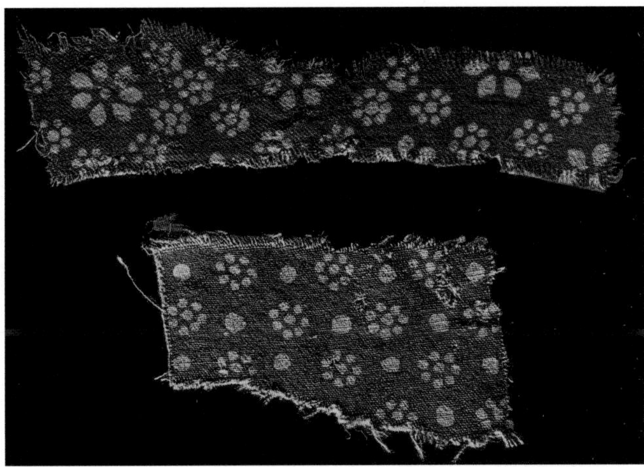

Fragments of a blue-ground printed batik from the Northern Dynasties period, unearthed in Xinjiang, China.

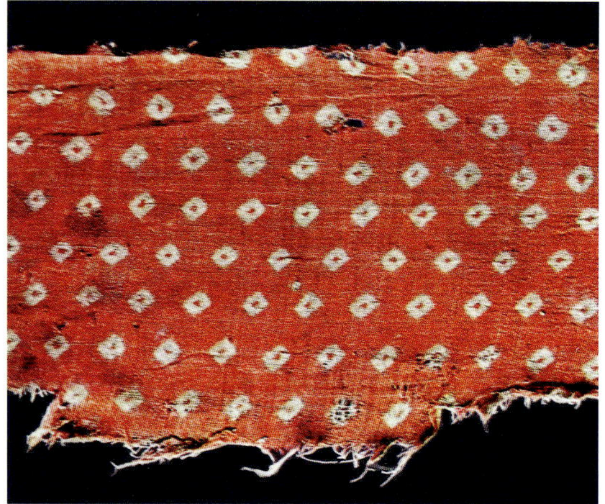

A fragment of red tie-dye silk from the Northern Dynasties period, unearthed in Xinjiang, China.

A fragment of green clamp-resist dyed silk from the Tang dynasty, unearthed in Xinjiang, China.

The image on the upper left, also from the Northern Dynasties period, depicts a red tie dye silk fragment, excavated from the ancient city ruins of Yutianwu Yulaike, Xinjiang. The red silk fabric is densely patterned with tie dye spots, forming regular circular square shapes, created by bundling threads to resist dye. The two fabric fragments belong to the same period, but the methods of resist dyeing are vastly different. During the Northern Dynasties period, a large number of fabric fragments dyed using tie dye and wax resistant techniques were discovered. By the Tang and Song dynasties, the tie dye, wax resistant, clamp resistant, and stencil printing techniques had become quite mature and were widely popular among the general public. In the Song dynasty, clamp resistant fabric became so widely used for military uniforms that it was prohibited for civilians to wear or sell. However, due to the widespread popularity of these fabrics among the people, the Southern Song (1127–1276) rulers had no choice but to lift the ban.

The image on the upper right shows a Tang dynasty printed silk skirt unearthed from the Astana tombs in Turpan of Xinjiang. The skirt depicts an image of an immortal riding a crane, flying through the sky, surrounded by flying birds, flowers, grass, mountains, water, and clouds. This is a piece created using the clamp resistant dyeing technique. The significant development of printing and dyeing technology during the Tang and Song dynasties led to a shift in fabric patterns from relatively simple and abstract designs to more detailed and complex ones. The popularity and prevalence of printed fabrics during this period is also reflected in many paintings and terracotta figurines. The image on the top of the facing page is Zhang Xuan's *Court Ladies Preparing Newly Woven Silk*. This painting depicts women of the Tang dynasty engaged in activities such as pounding raw silk, winding threads, ironing fabrics, and sewing. The long scroll features twelve figures, arranged in three groups, left, middle, and right. The large number of female garments depicted in the painting were created using wax resist and tie-dye techniques,

Court Ladies Preparing Newly Woven Silk, a Tang dynasty painting by Zhang Xuan.

Detail of the painting *Court Ladies Preparing Newly Woven Silk*.

among others.

The development of printing and dyeing technology, along with the expansion of East-West trade, allowed Chinese dyeing techniques to be introduced overseas. Techniques like block printing, indigo dyeing, and the use of indigo plants were transmitted to Japan during the Sui and Tang dynasties. Today, several pieces of Tang dynasty tie dye works are still preserved in the Shosoin Repository in Japan. Japan continues to maintain the most traditional forms of Chinese indigo dyeing, and it refers to this technique as "Tang dyeing."

During the Ming and Qing dynasties, different printing and dyeing methods became more refined, and the patterns that could be created became increasingly rich. For example, the *Suijin*, an ancient book compiling practical knowledge, records nine different variations of the clamp-resist dyeing technique. In stencil dyeing, blue printed cloth became extremely popular during the Qing dynasty and remains widely favored in China today, becoming a much-loved fabric for clothing among the general public.

Traditional Chinese plant dyeing techniques carry the wisdom and civilization of thousands of years. Every breakthrough in dyeing craftsmanship reflects the ancient artisans' exploration of nature's beauty and their dedication to preserving and passing down their craft. The continuous expansion of dye plants and color spectrum systems, along with the ongoing refinement of dyeing techniques, not only reflects the ancients' ultimate pursuit of color aesthetics but also highlights the profound heritage of Chinese civilization in both craftsmanship and cultural integration. As a vital representative of traditional Chinese craftsmanship, plant dyeing is not only a testament to history but also a cultural bridge that transcends time and space. In the present day, it continues to embody the ancient Eastern poetic expression of color and nature through its unique charm.

2. Characteristics and Sources of Plant Dyes

Plant dyeing is nature's gift to humanity. Currently, there are nearly 50 documented dyeing plants, along with approximately 200 more discovered through field investigations and experimental research, producing around 500 colors. Without these plants, our world of fabrics would lose its vibrant hues. Plant dyeing is the oldest, most environmentally friendly, and sustainable dyeing method used from ancient times to the present day.

Sources of Dyes

There is a wide variety of dyeing plants, with woody and herbaceous plants being the most common. Among the woody plants, trees are the most prevalent, followed by shrubs, while vine plants are less common. These plants span categories such as flowers, fruits, vegetables, and medicinal herbs. In particular, most of the plants introduced in Chapter Three of this book for dye extraction can also be used for medicinal purposes. Compared to mineral and animal dyes, plant dyes are richer in variety, more accessible, and can be recycled and regenerated.

Plant dyes are primarily extracted from the pigments found in various parts of plants, including flowers, leaves, stems, roots, fruits, and seeds. Some plants, such as Chinese indigo and Japanese knotweed, allow dye extraction from the entire plant. Certain plants have different parts that yield different colors, such as the leaves of the blue olive berry, which dye a yellow-brown, while the bark produces a black color. Other plants have specific parts that are used for dye extraction, such as the roots of the comfrey, which dye purple, and the amur cork tree, which dyes yellow.

Plants can be used for dyeing because they contain pigments. These pigments are dissolved in water, acidic, or alkaline solutions through processes such as boiling, and can then adhere relatively stably to fabrics. Every plant contains pigments, but not all pigments are capable of dyeing. Many freshly picked plants can have their juice transferred to fabric or paper through pounding, but only a portion of these pigments can achieve a relatively stable, long-lasting attachment. From a chemical structure perspective, plant dyeing mainly involves the following types of pigments, carotenoids, flavonoids, anthraquinones, naphthoquinones, polyphenols, diketones, indoles, alkaloids, and chlorophyll. Understanding the chemical structure of dyeing plants allows us to conduct more scientific research and reduces the occurrence of unpredictability in the dyeing process.

Factors Influencing the Dyeing Process

The existence and development of plant dyeing are closely tied to natural climate conditions. Traditional dyeing places great emphasis on seasonality, often using freshly harvested seasonal plants for dyeing. The ancient Chinese text *Rites of Zhou*, specifically the section on the *Offices of the Heaven*, records, "For dyeing, spring is for exposing the bleached fabric to the sun, summer for dyeing in light red and black, autumn for dyeing five colors, and winter for presenting the finished dyed fabrics as tribute for ceremonial use." Due to the varying climate of each season, dyeing tasks are divided according to the season. In spring, with warm weather, fabrics are pretreated, sun-dried, and boiled. Summer, with its heat, is ideal for dyeing dark colors, such as black. Autumn, with its moderate temperature and humidity, is the best season for large-scale dyeing work. Winter, however, with its cold weather, results in darker, less vibrant colors, making it less suitable for dyeing. Additionally, the pigment content in plants also varies by season. For example, the indigo plants have the highest pigment content just before they bloom in autumn, while in winter, their pigment content is at its lowest, making it almost impossible to extract dye.

Different geographical and climatic conditions, regional factors, and changes in air temperature and humidity all influence plant growth, which in turn directly affects the dyeing results. The trace elements present in the water quality of different regions can also alter the color outcomes. While it is ideal to align dyeing activities with favorable natural conditions, modern advancements in technology have allowed for better storage techniques for many plants. Additionally, the temperature, humidity, and other conditions of dyeing spaces have become more controllable, meaning that most plant dyeing is no longer limited by the seasons. Some plants, after being dried or processed into powder, can also be used for dyeing.

It is also important to mention that the wild growth of plants versus their cultivation can have a significant impact on dyeing, closely related to the accumulation of pigments over time. While wild-harvested dye plants are considered the best, cultivated plants can also meet dyeing requirements. Furthermore, wild plants have highly unstable yields, and their harvesting costs are relatively high. For example, a wild sappanwood used for dyeing requires hundreds of years to mature, whereas a cultivated version can grow to maturity in about 10 years, and its size is often much larger than that of the wild variety.

Diversity of Colors

Plant dyes can be broadly categorized into several color families, including red, yellow, blue, green, purple, black, and brown. Common plants used for dyeing red include sappanwood, safflower, madder and others. Plants for dyeing yellow include amur cork tree, gardenia, black locust flower, turmeric, wild turmeric and others. Various indigo plants, like Chinese indigo, Persian shield, true indigo, and woad, are popular for blue dyeing. Plants like comfrey and purple cabbage are used to create purple hues. Chinese nutgall, betel nut, Chinese sumac, tanoak, and hairy-fruited abacus plant are examples of plants used for black dyes. Plants such as tea leaves, walnut, pomegranate, green persimmon, and Chinese yam are used to produce brown shades. Green dyes are relatively rare. According to Chinese literature, only dahurian buckthorn can directly produce green, while other plants achieve green hues through repeated alternation of yellow and blue dyeing processes.

According to statistics, the most common dyeing plants are those that produce yellow colors, followed by red, blue, green, and black, with black being the least common. Among them, indigo is the most stable and prominent dye, especially in blue and all other dye categories. Indigo plants, which have high yields, provide a dye that can be processed into indigo mud, allowing it to be stored and used for a long time without being affected by seasonal changes in plant growth. This stability makes indigo dyeing the most widely used and widely spread in plant dyeing.

The above is a relatively broad classification, but each plant's dyeing effect has its own unique characteristics. For example, gardenia produces a more neutral yellow, while amur cork tree tends toward a lemon yellow. Additionally, many variables can affect the final dyeing result, primarily including the following

five factors.

1. As mentioned earlier, geographic and climatic conditions are uncontrollable factors. When dyeing, we need to align with nature and respect it.

2. Many plants can expand their color range when mixed with different mordants. For example, sappanwood can produce shades of orange-red, rose, purple-red, and deep purple when combined with different mordants, while amur cork tree can yield shades ranging from lemon yellow, yellow-green, to olive green. Using different mordants allows for the extraction of a wider variety of colors.

3. During the dyeing process, controlling the dyeing time, the ratio of dye to water (bath ratio), and the concentration of the dye can significantly affect the final color. The longer the dyeing time, the deeper the color, the larger the bath ratio, the lighter the color. The more concentrated the dye, the deeper the color. In Chinese, there is a saying, "Three alum, nine dyes." The "three alum" refer to different types of alum mordants, while "nine dyes" refers to multiple immersion cycles. The phrase conveys the idea that repeated dyeing or the more times the fabric is dyed, the deeper the color is.

4. Even when the same dye solution is used on thread and fabric, the resulting colors may differ. Different materials of fabric will also yield different final colors when dyed with the same solution. Generally, threads tend to absorb color more fully than fabrics. Fabrics with higher thread counts or thicker structures are harder to dye because the tight interlacing of the fibers makes it more difficult for the dye to penetrate compared to threads. As a result, the color on the fabric will appear lighter than that on the thread. Additionally, fabrics made from protein fibers, such as silk and wool, are easier to dye and tend to produce more vibrant colors than cellulose fiber fabrics like cotton, linen, or hemp.

5. Different dye solutions can be mixed to create new colors, a method that will be specifically introduced in Chapter Two on dyeing techniques. This greatly expands the color range of plant dyeing.

From top to bottom, the five pieces of dyed fabrics are colored respectively with sappanwood, betel nut, sappanwood, gardenia, and sappanwood.

Color samples dyed with sappanwood using different mordants.

Natural and Eco-Friendly

The biggest feature of plant dyes is their natural origin. The dyes come entirely from the plants themselves, and the extraction process generally has minimal environmental impact. Most of the modifiers are derived from plants and nature, such as alkaline modifier wood ash, which is a byproduct of burning straw and other plants, and acidic modifier smoked plum juice, which is obtained by decocting the fruit. Most mordants are natural alum-based minerals.

The wastewater produced during the dyeing process can be directly used for irrigation in farmlands, and the plant residues can become organic fertilizers. The process of extracting plant dyes does not easily cause environmental pollution, and the fabrics dyed with these dyes are healthier to use. Studies have shown that many chemical dyes not only pollute the environment during the dyeing process but can also produce carcinogenic substances during use, leading to their ban in some cases.

On the contrary, many plant dyes also have medicinal properties. During the dyeing process, the medicinal components can be absorbed by the fabric, offering health benefits. When used, these fabrics can help reduce potential health risks such as skin allergies and respiratory issues. As consumers become increasingly concerned with healthy lifestyles, the market demand for plant-dyed products has gradually grown. Some clothing brands are committed to using plant-dyed fabrics.

Drawbacks of Plant Dyeing

Of course, plant dyes also have certain drawbacks.

1. Compared to chemical dyes, the extraction process of plant dyes is relatively complicated, involving multiple steps. The dyeing process takes a longer time, and once the dye solution is extracted, it needs to be used within a short period. It's not easily stored and is prone to mold growth. This however, also partly proves the safety and environmental friendliness of plant dyes.

2. The stability and colorfastness of plant dyes are relatively poor. The dye molecules have lower reactivity, so when performing operations like folding fabric during dyeing, even without any anti-dye treatment, the parts that are folded or wrapped in the middle are very difficult to dye.

3. Plant dyes tend to be relatively expensive, especially when using high-quality medicinal plants or costly fruit and vegetable products. Some plants yield only a small amount of extractable pigment, which requires higher costs for dyeing.

4. Plant dyes cannot achieve precise color matching. It is difficult to replicate the exact same result across different batches of dyeing. However, this is also part of the charm of plant dyeing. Each attempt brings a new experience and surprise, allowing for the creation of unique, one-of-a-kind pieces.

In the process of modernization, although plant dyeing has inevitably been replaced by chemical dyeing, it still remains beloved for its unique handmade charm. Although the knowledge system of plant dyeing has become quite mature, it differs from industrial dyeing in that it is difficult to precisely control the color outcomes of each dyeing session. Many factors can affect the dyeing results, which is why it continues to captivate us, leading to ongoing exploration and the discovery of our own unique experiences. Some plants may not be the most commonly used for dyeing, but we can approach dyeing experiments with curiosity. There may be unexpected surprises. We can print and dye our own unique colors and fabrics, use the threads we've dyed for embroidery or weaving, and create home goods. Through the dyeing process, we can experience a harmonious connection with nature.

CHAPTER TWO

Preparations and Introduction to the Plant Dyeing Process

Plant dyeing is a very beginner-friendly craft and easy to get started with. However, for those who wish to study it systematically and in-depth, dyeing enthusiasts need to have a solid understanding of dye materials and techniques. They must also conduct extensive experiments and analyses to develop their own theoretical framework. The selection of each material and the execution of each process directly affect the final dyeing outcome. This chapter covers the necessary preparations before dyeing, introduces the materials involved, and explains the dyeing techniques. Additionally, it provides an analysis of the materials, tools, and fabric treatment methods required for the practical dyeing processes in Chapter Three and Four, serving as a foundation for the hands-on practice that follows.

1. Dyeing Tools

In natural dyeing, each stage of the process requires specific tools to ensure safety, accuracy, and effectiveness. This section introduces the tools used in extracting dye, carrying out handcraft printing and dyeing, and managing other essential tasks. You may already have some of these tools at home, or you can substitute them with items of similar function based on your needs.

Dye Extraction Tools

This section mainly introduces the tools needed for extracting dye liquid from plants. Many of the necessary tools for plant dyeing can be found in a household kitchen. However, it is advisable to avoid conducting dyeing processes in the kitchen to prevent contamination and accidental ingestion of dyes or mordants. Food utensils and dyeing tools should not be mixed to ensure safety during the process.

On the facing page
The tie-dye kerchief work using multiple plant dyeing techniques, resulting in rich colors and intricate patterns.

Steaming and boiling containers

Glass bottles and jars

Small containers, bowls, and plates

Induction cooker

Mesh strainers

Stirring rods

Clamp

Electronic scale

Spoons and strainers

Rubber gloves

Steaming and boiling containers: These barrels, pots, and basins are used for boiling or steaming plants to extract dye. They can be made of metal, ceramic, or glass and should be suitable for heating with an open flame or an induction cooker. The capacity is generally greater than 1,000 ml.

Glass bottles and jars: Used for storing dye liquids, dyes, and mordants. They should be airtight to allow for long-term storage.

Small containers, bowls, and plates: Open containers primarily used for cold dyeing liquids and for temporarily holding dye liquids, dyes, and mordants.

Induction cooker: A heating device for steaming and boiling plants. It can also be replaced with open-flame equipment such as natural gas or propane stoves.

Mesh strainer: A filtering tool used to separate plant materials from the dye liquid during extraction. It comes in various mesh sizes, allowing selection based on the size of plant particles.

Stirring rod: Used for stirring plants, fabrics, mordants, and other materials during dyeing. It can be made of metal, ceramic, plastic, or wood, but not glass.

Clamps: Used to remove fabric from the dye solution. They come in various materials and styles.

Electronic scale: Used to weigh plants, mordants, and water.

Spoons and strainers: Used for scooping fabric, plants, and dye solutions. The appropriate specifications can be chosen based on the different situations.

Rubber gloves: Used when handling dyes, mordants, or dyed fabrics, effectively preventing hands from being stained by dyes and mordants.

Handcraft Printing and Dyeing Tools

In dyeing, using different resist techniques can create a variety of rich patterns. The tools involved are numerous. This section will introduce only the tools involved in the creative works presented in Chapter Four of the book. During the creative process, you can also choose and adjust the tools listed below, or use similar products with the same function.

Tie-Dye Tools

Wooden boards: These are resist-dyeing tools used in tie-dyeing. Two wooden boards of the same shape and size are used to clamp the fabric that has been folded or manipulated. The parts of the fabric clamped by the wood will be resistant to the dye, preventing the dye from penetrating, and ultimately forming distinct patterns. The different shapes of the wooden boards can produce different pattern effects. Additionally, the dyed wooden boards can be reused, although they may leave residual color on the new fabric, resulting in unexpected color textures. Wooden boards can be purchased directly or custom-cut according to individual needs.

Clips: These are resist-dyeing tools, which can include metal clips, wooden

Wooden boards

Clips

Strings, ropes, and rubber bands

Round sticks and tubes

clips, plastic clips, G-clamps, paper clips, etc. The parts of the fabric clamped by the clips are protected from dyeing, leaving various impressions and patterns on the fabric where the clips are applied.

Strings, ropes, and rubber bands: These are resist-dyeing tools made from strong materials like cotton, linen, or plastic, which are durable and not easily broken. Thicker ropes are used to tie fabric, and after tying, the rope leaves marks of the same thickness on the fabric where dye cannot penetrate. Finer strings are used for sewing fabric. Both types effectively block the dye from penetrating. The tying ropes or strings can be reused, and when used again, they may transfer residual dye from the previous dyeing to the new fabric.

Round sticks and tubes: These are auxiliary tools for tie-dyeing. Fabric can be wrapped around a stick or other cylindrical material for the tying process. Different thicknesses of tubes can be chosen based on the size of the fabric being dyed. Materials like wood, glass, or PVC are all suitable for these tools.

Wax Dyeing Tools

Wax knife and wax pot: Tools for applying wax. Wax knives are typically made by layering copper or aluminum sheets and clamping them together. The larger the knife, the more layers it has, allowing for more wax storage. The shape is mainly fan-shaped or trapezoidal. Wax pots have a boat-shaped spout and a larger wax storage capacity than the wax knife. The wax flows out through a curved tube, and the finer the tube, the less wax flows out, allowing for more intricate designs. In addition to wax pots and wax knives, homemade tools such as sticks and stamps can also be used to apply wax.

Boar bristle brush: A brush used for drawing wax, capable of creating a hand-painted brushstroke effect. It is made of boar bristles.

Wax: A resist-dyeing tool, available in two types, paraffin wax and beeswax, which can also be mixed in certain proportions. Paraffin wax is extracted from petroleum, with a melting point of about 45–60°C. It is relatively hard and has low adhesive strength, making it prone to cracking and allowing dye penetration during the dyeing process, creating a crackle effect on the fabric. Beeswax, secreted by bees, is a fatty substance with a yellow color and stronger stickiness, with a melting point of 62–66°C. By mixing both in different ratios, one can combine the advantages and disadvantages of each. In the image, from left to right, are paraffin wax, beeswax, and mixed wax. In addition to wax, plant-extracted substances like maple resin, pine resin, and sticky plant gum, which have strong adhesive properties, can also be used as resist agents.

Small electric stove and wax melting pot: Wax melting equipment that maintains a constant temperature and heat. It can be placed on a tabletop, making it convenient for use when drawing wax-dyed patterns. A stainless-steel melting pot is suitable as it can be placed directly on the small electric stove for heating.

Wax knives and wax pots

Boar bristle brushes

Wax

Small electric stove and wax melting pot

Stencil Printing Tools

Scraper: Used for spreading resist paste on fabric. It can be made from waterproof materials such as plastic or metal. The edge of the scraper should be smooth, and the appropriate size should be selected based on the dimensions of the stencils.

Carving knife: A tool used for carving the pattern stencil. It has a slanted blade and a sharp tip.

Brush: Used for applying tung oil to the kraft paper. You can choose a brush head with a relatively stiff bristle, such as nylon, boar bristle, or wolf hair. The size of the brush should be chosen based on the dimensions of the kraft paper.

Tung oil: Extracted from the seeds of the tung tree, tung oil is a high-quality drying plant oil. It is commonly used in the creation of stencils for stencil printing. When applied to kraft paper, tung oil makes the paper waterproof and resistant to wear, enhancing the durability of the stencil.

Kraft paper: Used for making pattern stencils, with a thickness of 0.5 to 1 millimeter. A pattern stencil is a hollow template used in stencil printing. The design is drawn on the kraft paper and then carved out. The hollowed-out areas are revealed as patterns when the stencil paste is applied to resist dyeing during the printing process.

Other Tools

In addition to tools directly used for dyeing, some general-purpose tools are also helpful for measuring, marking, and cutting during preparation and design. These tools can be selected and adjusted according to your personal working habits or project requirements.

Pens: Used for drawing on fabric. It is recommended to use erasable pens. The three pens on the left in the image are heat-erasable pens. The ink will disappear automatically at high temperatures. The two pens on the right are water-erasable pens. The ink will disappear when exposed to water. Different types of pens can be selected based on the temperature conditions or water exposure during the dyeing process.

Scrapers

Carving knife set

Brushes

Tung oil

Kraft paper

Hand sewing needles: Embroidery needles can be used. They come in various thicknesses with different-sized eye holes. Select the appropriate needle size based on the thickness of the sewing thread.

Pin needles: Used to secure fabric during sewing. The image shows hand-sewing pin needles, but if using a sewing machine, flat-head machine pins can also be used.

Compass: Used for drawing circular guide lines.

Handheld steam iron: Used for pressing fabrics. It is not recommended to use a hanging steamer. Ensure that excess dye is thoroughly washed out before ironing to prevent staining the iron's base and contaminating other fabrics. For wax dyeing, if the iron is used for wax removal, it is advisable to have a dedicated iron for this purpose.

Ruler: Used for drawing the edges of dyeing patterns. It is recommended to use a professional quilting ruler, as shown in the image. This ruler has horizontal and vertical lines marked at 1 cm intervals, allowing for more precise drawing of right angles and parallel lines.

Scissors: Used for cutting fabric and thread. For tying and sewing threads, it is recommended to use small, pointed scissors for precision.

Rotary cutter and cutting mat: Used for cutting fabric. Place the fabric on the cutting mat and use the rotary cutter along with a ruler to cut the fabric. This tool is more accurate and efficient than scissors and allows for cutting multiple fabric layers at once.

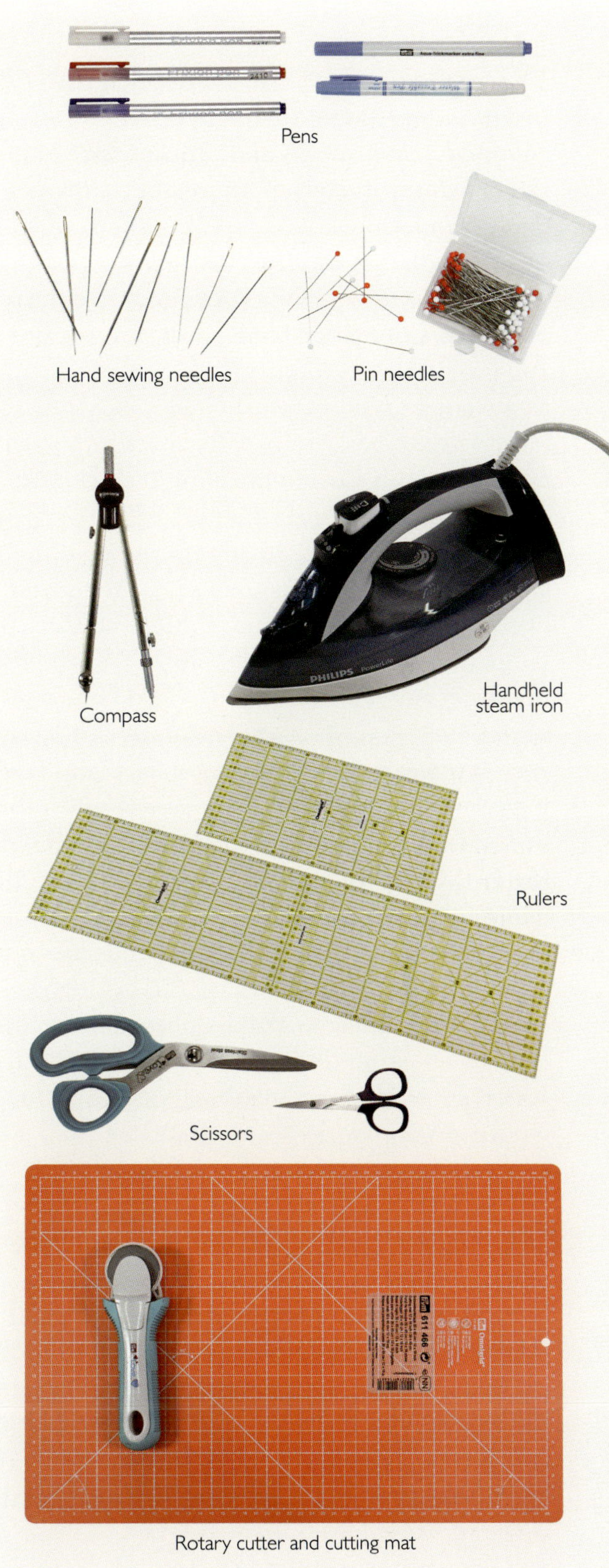

Pens

Hand sewing needles

Pin needles

Compass

Handheld steam iron

Rulers

Scissors

Rotary cutter and cutting mat

2. Dyeing Fabrics

The textile fibers we use are divided into two main categories, natural fibers and synthetic fibers. Synthetic fibers are artificial. They contain many chemical components and require special processing techniques. Dyeing is carried out using either atmospheric pressure or high temperature and high pressure methods, which makes them unsuitable for hand dyeing. For hand dyeing, only natural fiber fabrics are used, which include cellulose fibers and protein fibers. Cellulose fibers are derived from plants and are mainly extracted from plant seeds, bast, leaves, and fruits like cotton, linen, ramie, and bark fibers. Protein fibers come from animals and are obtained from their hair or secretions, such as silk, wool, cashmere, rabbit hair, and yak hair. These fibers are usually spun into yarn first, and then processed into fabric through various weaving techniques.

The thickness and tightness of the yarn, as well as the thickness and density of the fabric, all affect how well the dye is absorbed. Yarns vary in twist level. The higher the twist, the tighter and more compact the yarn becomes. The thicker and tighter the yarn, the more difficult and slower it is for the dye to penetrate. Fabric is formed by the interweaving of yarns in the warp and weft directions. Two key factors influence this process. The specifications of the yarn, especially its twist level, and the thread count, which refers to the number of warp and weft threads per square inch. The higher the thread count, the denser and more tightly woven the fabric becomes. The more tightly the warp and weft threads are interwoven, the lower the dye uptake rate, and the slower the dyeing process becomes. Therefore, even fabrics made from the same material can show differences in hue during the dyeing process, especially cotton. Beginners are encouraged to experiment with a variety of fabric types and yarn specifications, making small test samples to build a personal dyeing reference archive. This will help in selecting the most suitable textiles for future creative projects. This section provides explanation specifically focusing on cotton, linen, silk, and wool, and the works featured in this book are all made using these types of fabrics.

Cotton

Cotton fabric and cotton yarn are textiles made from the seed fibers of the cotton plant. These fibers contain up to 95% cellulose, which is the primary material used in the production of cotton textiles. Based on fiber length and thickness, cotton fibers can be categorized into Upland cotton, Pima cotton, and Levant cotton.

Among them, Upland cotton has finer fibers with moderate strength and is the most widely cultivated type of cotton worldwide. Pima cotton has fine and long fibers with higher strength and is considered the highest quality variety. Levant cotton, on the other hand, has short, thick fibers with lower strength and inferior quality. many regions have stopped cultivating it and it is generally not used to produce cotton fabric directly. Instead, it is typically processed through chemical methods to create blended fibers.

Cotton fibers are typically off white or pale yellow in color, and the fabrics made from them retain this natural hue. Such unprocessed cotton fabric is known as greige fabric or natural white cotton. There is also bleached cotton fabric, which appears cleaner and purer in color, free from particles like cotton shells, and tends to have a cool or warm white tone. In recent years, naturally colored cotton varieties have been cultivated, but they are mostly Levant cotton types, with unstable yields and inconsistent pigmentation. The cotton fabric we use for dyeing primarily consists of greige fabric and bleached cotton. Cotton textiles have excellent breathability, water absorbency, and abrasion resistance. Among natural fibers, cotton is the most affordable and is the most widely used.

Linen

Linen textiles are derived from the bast fibers and leaf fibers of plants. Bast fibers include ramie, flax, jute, and kenaf, with ramie and flax being of the highest quality. Leaf fibers include sisal and abacá, and they are extracted from the leaf veins and leaf sheaths of plants. Compared to bast fibers, leaf fibers are more rigid and are referred to as "hard fibers." The hardness of linen fibers is generally higher than that of cotton fibers. Linen feels rougher to the touch, has lower elasticity, and is more prone to wrinkles. However, linen fibers are extremely strong, highly moisture absorbent, and possess excellent properties such as high-temperature resistance, corrosion resistance, acid and alkali resistance, and abrasion resistance.

Silk

Silk fibers are the secretion produced by the silkworm's salivary glands. Before transforming from larva to pupa, the baby silkworm continuously secretes layers of silk to wrap around its body, forming an oval shaped cocoon to protect itself during the metamorphosis process. The silkworm cocoon is the raw material for silk fabrics. During the entire process of silk secretion, the silk produced by the silkworm never breaks. The cocoon formed can be softened by boiling—a process called "reeling"—which allows a single long strand of silk to be extracted. This is the only long fiber among natural fibers, typically ranging in length from 800 to 1,200 meters.

Silkworms can be divided into two types, domesticated and wild. Domesticated silkworms produce the highest quality silk. Wild silkworms, such as tussah and castor silkworms, have more difficult reeling processes and produce lower quality silk. Silk is white and semi-transparent in appearance. Compared to cotton, linen, and wool fabrics, it is the lightest in texture, with the strongest sheen, and is fine, soft, smooth, and elastic. The texture of silk is closest to human skin, earning it the nickname "the second skin." However, silk has poor light resistance and should not be exposed to direct sunlight. Prolonged sun exposure can cause the protein fibers to harden, become damaged, and lead to yellowing and aging of the fabric.

Wool

There are many types of animal fibers, such as wool, cashmere, rabbit hair, mohair, yak hair, mink fur, and more. Among these, wool is the most commonly used, with sheep wool being the most prevalent.

Wool can be classified based on its thickness and length into fine wool, superfine wool, and coarse wool. The quality of sheep wool varies depending on the season it is sheared. Wool sheared in the spring is of higher quality because the fibers are finer, there is more lanolin, and the fleece is denser.

Wool fibers are naturally curly and relatively long, with scales on their surface. When friction occurs, the scales interlock and cause felting. Therefore, excessive rubbing and washing of wool fabrics can lead to felting and shrinkage. Wool fibers have lower strength compared to cotton fibers, but they possess excellent elasticity and strong plasticity. Alkaline agents are damaging to wool, so care should be taken when using certain dyes that contain alkaline substances during dyeing. Wool has excellent moisture absorbency and warmth retention, and it is resistant to soiling. However, due to its protein fiber composition, wool is prone to moth damage, and its smoothness can deteriorate when exposed to moisture. Therefore, it is important to store wool in a dry, pest free environment.

3. Pre- and Post-Dyeing Treatments

The pre-dyeing and post-dyeing treatments primarily target the dyed material. Since the material contains impurities such as sizing and gums, these can affect the dyeing speed, brightness, and hue. For different types of yarns and fabrics, specific pre-dyeing treatments and post-dyeing fixation processes are required.

Pre-Dyeing Treatment for Cotton and Linen

Before weaving, cotton and linen fibers are often coated with sizing on the yarn to enhance smoothness and strength. The sizing can block the contact between the dye pigments and the fabric, slowing down the dyeing process and reducing the brightness of the color. Therefore, a desizing treatment is required before dyeing to remove the sizing.

Step 1: Prepare a container that can be used for steaming or boiling, and add an appropriate amount of clean water. The water level should be sufficient to fully submerge the fabric or yarn.

Step 2: Heat the water until steam begins to rise, then place the fabric into the water. Stir the water while it heats. If working with yarn, to prevent the yarn from tangling or knotting during stirring, insert a round stick through the middle of the yarn. Place the stick across the container, and rotate the yarn in segments into the heated water. As the yarn heats up, you can use another round stick to assist with the rotation.

Step 3: Maintain the water at a boiling state and heat for 5 to 10 minutes, continuously stirring the fabric or yarn to ensure it fully interacts with the water. During this time, the sizing will dissolve into the water, causing the water to become murky.

Step 4: Remove the fabric or yarn from the water and rinse it thoroughly under clean water, repeating the process until the water runs clear. Wring out excess water and either hang it to dry or use an iron to smooth it out.

Pre-Dyeing Treatment for Silk and Wool

Silk fabrics and yarns available in the market are classified into raw silk and processed silk. Raw silk contains sericin, a natural gum, and has not undergone a degumming process. It is relatively stiff and is typically used for fabrics such as raw silk fabric, gauze, or as weft yarn in weaving.

Processed silk has undergone a degumming treatment, removing the gum and impurities, making it softer, more skin-friendly, and with a stronger luster. Processed silk is generally used for weaving fabrics like chiffon, organza, crepe, satin, and others of various thicknesses. Chinese Shu brocade and Song brocade are both made using processed silk, while Yun brocade uses processed silk for the warp and raw silk for the weft.

Both raw and processed silk can be dyed, but under the same conditions, raw silk absorbs dye more deeply, resulting in a darker color with a matte finish. Processed silk, on the other hand, takes on a lighter color with a stronger luster, producing a glossy appearance. The choice can be made based on the creator's specific needs. If processed silk is used, no pre-treatment is required. However, if raw silk is to be transformed into processed silk, it needs to undergo a treatment. During the degumming process of raw silk, not all the sericin is removed. For everyday, skin friendly fabrics, a 75% degumming rate is sufficient.

Wool fibers also contain natural gum and require a degumming process. Wool purchased in the market is generally already degummed. If untreated wool is used, the degumming process is the same as that for silk. Due to wool's natural curl, after degumming, the fibers will straighten out from their curled form.

Step 1: Prepare a container suitable for steaming or boiling and add an appropriate amount of clean water. Ensure there is enough water to fully submerge the fabric or thread.

Step 2: Add wood ash or soda ash to the clean water, with a ratio of 3–5% of the textile's weight. Alternatively, you can use pH test strips to check that the pH value is between 10 and 11. Since soda ash tends to clump in cold water, it can first be dissolved in warm water before being added to the clean water.

Step 3: After adding wood ash to water, the potassium carbonate molecules will precipitate and dissolve in the water. The wood ash itself does not completely dissolve in water. Therefore, if using wood ash, to prevent ash particles from sticking to the fabric and complicating the post-treatment cleaning, you can let the wood ash water sit for two days. This allows the potassium carbonate molecules in the ash to dissolve into the water. Afterward, filter the ash residue using a fine sieve, retaining only the clear solution at the top. If using soda ash, this step is not necessary.

Step 4: Heat the wood ash water or soda ash water until it starts steaming, and then place the fabric or yarn into the water. Stir while heating. To prevent the yarn from tangling or knotting during stirring, you can thread a round stick through the middle of the yarn, and place the stick on top of the container. Rotate the yarn in sections into the water for boiling. As the yarn heats up, you can use an additional round stick to assist with the rotation.

Step 5: Keep the water at a boiling state and heat for 1 to 2 hours, periodically stirring the fabric or yarn to ensure it thoroughly blends with the water.

Step 6: Remove the fabric or yarn from the water, rinse thoroughly 5 to 6 times, then wring out the excess water. Leave it to air dry indoors in the shade, or use a hairdryer to dry it.

From left to right, cotton threads dyed with sappanwood (groups 1–2), amur cork tree (groups 3–5), and betel nut (group 6).

Post-Dyeing Color Fixation

After plant dyeing, a large amount of pigment molecules will adhere to the fabric surface. It is necessary to wash the fabric multiple times to remove the excess dye, until the water runs clear with no remaining pigment. If the excess dye is not thoroughly washed out, it could cause the fabric to lose color when it comes into contact with water, and the excess dye may transfer onto other items it touches. After the excess dye has been washed out, some fading may still occur during the subsequent use and cleaning of the fabric. This is a normal phenomenon.

The color fastness varies depending on the type of plant dye used, and the degree of fading will differ. Therefore, fabric is typically treated with a color fixation process after dyeing. Traditional plant dyeing generally does not involve color fixation for light colored fabrics, but deep colored fabrics are treated to prevent rapid fading. When processing cotton fibers, a solution is made by dissolving 3–5% of the fabric's weight in edible salt in water. The mixture is heated to around 50°C, and the fabric is soaked for 1 to 2 hours to help fix the color.

For processing linen, silk, and wool fibers, an acid agent such as edible vinegar or smoked plum juice is used, diluted with water to maintain a pH value between 3 to 5. The solution is heated to around 50°C, and the fabric is soaked for 1 to 2 hours. Alternatively, professional fabric color fixatives can be purchased, which typically offer a colorfastness rating of 4 to 5. However, most color fixative products are chemical based, so readers should use them with discretion depending on the specific circumstances.

Storage of Dye Liquids

Dye liquids should follow the principle of "use immediately after preparation" and should not be stored for long periods. Some fabrics have higher dyeing requirements, and if dyeing cannot be completed within one day, fresh dye liquid should be extracted the following day to continue the process.

Dye liquids stored at room temperature will gradually mold over time due to the presence of microorganisms in the extracted dye liquid. Even when sealed, the storage can only slow down the molding process, not prevent it entirely. In the summer, dye liquids stored at room temperature for 3 to 5 days will develop noticeable mold spots. Adding mordants to the dye liquid can help slow down the molding process. Dye liquids that have started to mold can still be used for dyeing, but the color will not be as vibrant as with fresh dye liquid, and there may be slight changes in the hue. Therefore, it is recommended to extract the appropriate amount of dye liquid based on the fabric's weight and the desired depth of color when using dye liquids.

4. Dye Mordants

Not all plants in nature can be used for dyeing, and even those that can may have weak adhesion of the extracted pigments to fabrics. To stabilize and accelerate the attachment of the dye molecules to the fibers, mordants are used to create a chemical reaction between the dye and the fabric. As a dyeing medium, mordants not only enhance the absorption and color fastness of the dye but also, depending on the type of mordant used, can produce different colors from the same dye.

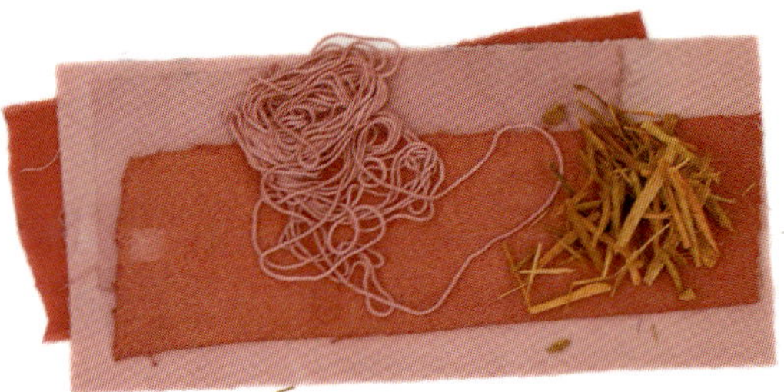

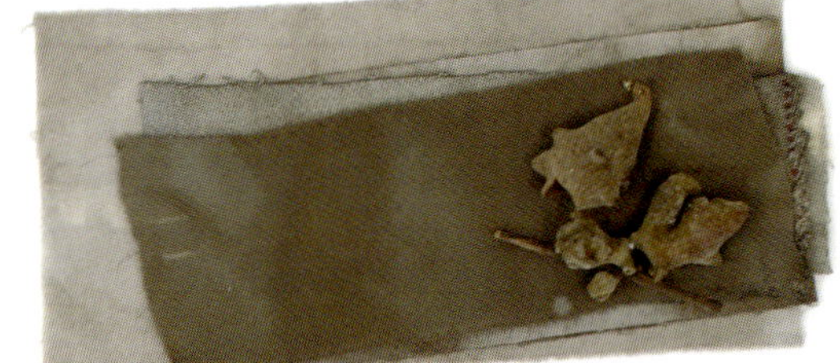

From top to bottom, plant dye color samples of gardenia, amur cork tree, sappanwood, purple gromwell, nutgall, and betel nut.

Mordants include natural mordants and chemical mordants. Natural mordants are environmentally friendly and generally derived from nature. They can be used in the processing of everyday products and food. Chemical mordants, on the other hand, are obtained through chemical purification and, although some originate from nature, they contain trace amounts of heavy metals that can harm both the body and the environment if used long term.

Here are some common natural mordants:

Wood ash: This is the ash powder produced from burning dry grass, straw, or dry tree branches. It can be bought or made by oneself through burning and refining. Wood ash is an alkaline agent, and its main component is potassium carbonate. Wood ash itself is not soluble in water, but potassium carbonate dissolves in water. You can place wood ash in water, let it settle, and then filter to extract the water solution for use, or it can be directly dissolved in water for dyeing. Wood ash has a mild alkalinity, medicinal properties, and is also an important mordant for dyeing black.

Lime powder: This is a natural rock containing calcium carbonate that is heated to high temperatures to produce a white powder. It is an alkaline substance used in construction, agriculture, food industry, and environmental protection. There are two types, quicklime (raw lime powder) and slaked lime powder. For dyeing, quicklime is used, while slaked lime powder has a stronger alkalinity and can cause skin burns if used improperly, so it should be avoided. Its function is similar to that of wood ash, as both are alkaline agents, but lime powder is more alkaline than wood ash, so it is recommended to use wood ash as the first choice.

Baking soda: Composed of sodium carbonate and appears as a white powder. It is highly soluble at high temperatures and, when dissolved in water, creates a strong alkaline solution. It is commonly used in daily life for baking, particularly in dough preparation, and for frying foods.

Acidic agents: Substances like smoked plum juice, bayberry juice, and vinegar contain acidic compounds and can be used as acid agents. The juices from smoked plums and bayberry can be extracted by boiling the fruits and using the resulting liquid for dyeing purposes.

Alum: This is an aluminum ion mordant, processed from sulfate minerals and typically appears as transparent or semi-transparent crystals.

Green vitriol: This is an iron ion mordant, primarily composed of ferrous sulfate, and is made by roasting yellow iron ore. It reacts with plants containing tannin to produce a blue black color. Historically, it was commonly used for dyeing deep or black shades.

Yellow alum: This is a sulfate mineral, primarily composed of iron sulfate, and typically appears in crystal or powder form. It is another form of copperas (green vitriol). When green vitriol undergoes sedimentation, its color changes from green to yellow. Both yellow and green copperas have the same composition and are commonly used as mordants for dyeing dark colors. The color result from the same dye may slightly differ depending on the form of copperas used.

Blue vitriol: This is a copper ion mordant, characterized by its blue crystalline sulfate form. Like the other four types of vitriol minerals, blue vitriol is also used in medicinal applications. However, it is important to note that these minerals can be toxic. When using them, it's essential to wear gloves and a mask to avoid ingestion.

Iron slurry: This is a solution containing iron elements, commonly used as a key mordant for dyeing black. It is produced by rusting metal iron with water or vinegar. Rusting with water takes a relatively long time, usually requiring at least 7 to 10 days, but adding hydrogen peroxide can speed up the process. A notable example of using iron slurry is the traditional Chinese fabric, Gambiered Guangdong gauze (*Xiangyunsha* silk), which is dyed using naturally iron-rich river mud from Guangdong as a mordant.

5. Dyeing Process

The plant dyeing process is divided into two main categories. One involves extracting dye liquid from plants to dye the fabric. Plant dyes can be used for direct dyeing or can be dyed together with mordants. This method of dyeing can result in solid colors or fabrics with gradient or ombre effects. If you want to create figurative or abstract patterns on fabric, another type of dyeing process is required, which involves resist dyeing or printing techniques. Resist dyeing refers to using different materials or tools to block dye from certain areas of the fabric, which can be further subdivided into methods such as tie dye, wax resistant dyeing, and clamp resistant dyeing. Printing involves using carved molds to apply dye to the fabric through stamping or pressing.

Direct Dyeing

All plant dyes obtained through extraction can be directly used for dyeing. Some dyes produce relatively lighter colors, such as Chinese nutgall, which gives a pale grayish white color when directly dyed. However, when a mordant is added, it can produce a deep black color. In general, the colors dyed with a mordant are darker than those dyed with dye liquor that does not contain a mordant. Direct dyeing generally involves soaking the fabric for 2 to 4 hours. Prolonged soaking does not deepen the color of the fabric, and instead, multiple immersions are required to achieve a deeper color.

After the first soak, the fabric is removed and air-dried, then reintroduced into the dye for a second round of dyeing. This process is repeated several times until the desired color depth is achieved. Each plant dye has a specific color range. For example, gardenia dye produces a yellow color, and the depth of color achieved through multiple immersions will range from light yellow to bright yellow, but it cannot be dyed to a deep yellow.

The stencil-dyed kerchief work infused with the brightness and vitality of spring.

Mordanting

Adding different mordants to plant dyes can result in changes in the brightness, purity, and hue of the color. For example, the color range of sappanwood is quite broad, and adding various mordants can produce shades ranging from orange-red, scarlet, bright red, purple, deep purple, to nearly black. By contrast, dyes like gardenia and amur cork tree, which are used for yellow hues, exhibit fewer changes when mordants are added.

The mordanting method has various application techniques depending on the plant used. Typically, the plant dye is first extracted, and then a mordant is added for dyeing. Additionally, the mordant can be mixed with the dye bath and used together for dyeing. In this case, the fabric can simply be immersed directly into the dye bath. The mordant can also be dissolved in clean water to prepare a separate mordant solution. During dyeing, the fabric is first immersed in the mordant solution and then placed into the dye bath for immersion, repeating the process in cycles. Compared to the previous method, this later dyeing technique is slower but allows for better absorption of the dye. For light colors, both methods can be used, but for dark colors, the latter method is recommended.

The tie-dye kerchief work in vibrant shades of orange, capturing the lively energy of summer.

In addition to the method of extracting the dye bath first and then adding the mordant, some plants require the mordant to be added during the extraction process in order to produce the color. Examples of such plants include Chinese nutgall, betel nut, safflower, and purple gromwell. The dyeing methods for these plants will be explained in detail in Chapter Three on dye extraction.

Over Dyeing

The rich variety of colors in plant dyeing is not solely achieved through individual plant pigments and mordants. Another method involves over dyeing with two different dyes to create new colors. This technique differs from mixing paint colors in painting, as plant dyes cannot simply be blended together. This is because different plant dyes require different pH levels for effective dyeing. Instead, the dyes must be applied in succession, for example, dyeing the fabric in a yellow dye bath first, then rinsing and drying it before immersing it in a blue dye bath. The final result is a green color.

The over dyeing method of alternating dyes results in progressively deeper colors. This process is fundamentally different from color blending in painting. For example, in painting, gray can be created by mixing white and black. However, in fabric dyeing, once a fabric has been dyed a dark color, it cannot be lightened by over dyeing with a lighter dye. Therefore, if a design includes multiple colors, it is essential to plan the dyeing sequence in advance and apply the colors from light to dark.

Resist Dyeing and Printing

Resist dyeing is a technique applied on the basis of dyeing, where different tools or materials are used to block specific areas of the fabric, preventing the dye from penetrating those sections. The unblocked areas absorb the dye and become colored, while the resisted areas remain uncolored or take on only a slight tint depending on the effectiveness of the resist, thus forming distinct patterns.

Traditional Chinese resist dyeing is known as *xie* (tying a knot). **Tie dyeing** is a resist technique that involves partially or fully binding or stitching the fabric using tools such as wooden pieces, clips, or string. Folding and binding the fabric with these tools can produce regular geometric patterns. String binding leaves textured marks on the fabric where the string was tied, while stitching leaves small puncture marks where the needle passed through the fabric. The direction and style of stitching also influence the resulting pattern.

Batik, or wax resistant dyeing, makes use of the property of wax to melt at high temperatures and solidify quickly at room temperature. Typically, wax is applied to the fabric as a resist material before dyeing. After dyeing is complete, the wax is removed using high heat. Wax-resist dyeing is well suited for representational patterns. Using different tools to apply the wax results in a variety of textured effects.

Clamp resistant dyeing involves printing with carved wooden blocks. It is essentially a type of stencil dyeing, where folded fabric is clamped between two carved wooden plates. These plates use concave carving, and the uncarved areas press tightly against the fabric. Dye penetrates only through the carved-out areas, creating the desired pattern.

Grey resistant dyeing uses paper stencils with cut out patterns, applying a resist paste by brushing it over the stencil to prevent dye from penetrating those areas, also known as Blue Calico. Another method involves using woodblocks with convex carvings, which are dipped directly into dye and pressed onto the fabric. This belongs to the category of printing techniques.

Each resist dyeing technique has a long history of tradition and a well-developed, systematic production process, which cannot be fully explained in just a few sentences. Chapter Four of this book, on dyeing applications, provides detailed introductions and practical uses of these resist techniques. It is recommended that beginners first become proficient in these foundational methods before moving on to their own creative work.

CHAPTER THREE

Plant Dyes and Their Dyeing Effects

The types of dye pigments contained in plants vary. Some pigments dissolve directly in water and can be extracted using the boiling method, while others dissolve in acids, alkalis, or alcohols and require different extraction methods to be processed for dyeing. There are many types of dye plants, and this book introduces nine of the most widely used and easily extractable plants in traditional Chinese dyeing. These plants cover six major color categories, red, yellow, blue, purple, brown, and black.

1. Red Series: Sappanwood

Sappanwood is a small tree belonging to the legume family. It is native to India, Myanmar, and Vietnam, with cultivation also found in China's Yunnan, Guizhou, and Fujian provinces. Sappanwood has a wide range of uses. Its heartwood serves as both a dyeing material and a medicinal ingredient and can also be used as a food additive. When using sappanwood for dyeing, the heartwood is typically sawed and split into thin slices, then further cut into strips to facilitate pigment extraction during boiling.

When used medicinally, sappanwood can be ground into powder for external application, offering benefits such as promoting blood circulation, reducing bruising, alleviating swelling, and relieving pain. Sappanwood's ability to dye fabrics comes from its heartwood, which contains a high concentration of brazilin. This pigment is initially colorless but oxidizes into brazilein, a reddish dye that is highly water-soluble. It adheres well to both protein and cellulose fibers. Sappanwood has a broad dyeing spectrum, and when combined with different mordants, it produces a rich variety of hues, ranging from orange-red and bright red to deep red and purplish-red, with varying shades of intensity.

On the facing page
The tie-dye tote bag in shades of deep blue and gray, echoing the calm of the sky.

1

2

3

4

5

6

7

8

Dye Extraction and Effects

Step 1:

Mix 250 g of sappanwood with 1,500 ml of clean water in a pot. Bring the mixture to a boil over high heat, then reduce to a simmer and continue boiling for 30 minutes. Stir the sappanwood frequently during this process to ensure maximum pigment extraction into the water to conduct the first extraction. Keep the pot covered tightly to prevent excessive evaporation.

Step 2:

Use a filter bowl or a fine mesh strainer to filter the dye liquid obtained after boiling, removing the remaining sappanwood residue. The fine mesh strainer will effectively filter out small impurities, preventing them from adhering to fabric or threads during the dyeing process, which could be difficult to clean later.

Step 3:

Pour the filtered sappanwood back into the pot and repeat Step 1 for a second round of extraction. After two rounds of boiling, the pigment from the sappanwood will be mostly extracted.

Step 4:

Combine the dye liquids from Step 2 and Step 3. This will give you approximately 3,000 ml of dye liquid.

Step 5:

Divide the 3,000 ml of extracted dye evenly into 5 containers and prepare the mordant mixture. For each 1,000 ml of dye liquid, add 3 to 5 g of the respective mordant, and stir the dye continuously to ensure the mordant completely dissolves. As the mordant dissolves, the dye will take on different colors. In this dyeing process, the dye is mixed with the original liquid and four different mordants to create color samples. From left to right, the samples are, sappanwood original liquid, alum mordant solution, yellow alum mordant solution, copper sulphate mordant solution, and ferrous sulphate mordant solution.

Step 6:

Place cotton, linen, cashmere, and silk fabrics separately into the dye solutions. For cotton and linen fabrics, a pretreatment is necessary. Refer to Chapter Two (page 35) for details. Boil the fabric in hot water to remove impurities and natural resins. After pretreatment, soak the fabric in water to dampen it before placing it into the dye solution. Let the fabrics soak at room temperature for 2 to 4 hours. Keep stirring the fabrics in the first ten minutes to ensure that the fabrics absorb the pigment of the dyeing solution evenly, and stir the fabrics frequently during the process. After the soaking period, remove the fabrics one by one.

Step 7:

After mordanting, remove the fabric from the dye solution and rinse it thoroughly to remove any floating dye. Gently wring out the excess water and hang the fabric to air dry. Once the fabric is partially or fully dry, you can iron it to smooth out wrinkles if desired.

Step 8:

After dyeing, organize and archive the fabric samples and threads, recording the corresponding values and quantities used. During future dyeing projects, refer to these color samples to choose the appropriate fabric and mordant for artistic creation.

Dye Color Samples

Sappanwood original liquid

Sappanwood + alum

Sappanwood + copper sulphate

Sappanwood + ferrous sulphate

Sappanwood + yellow alum

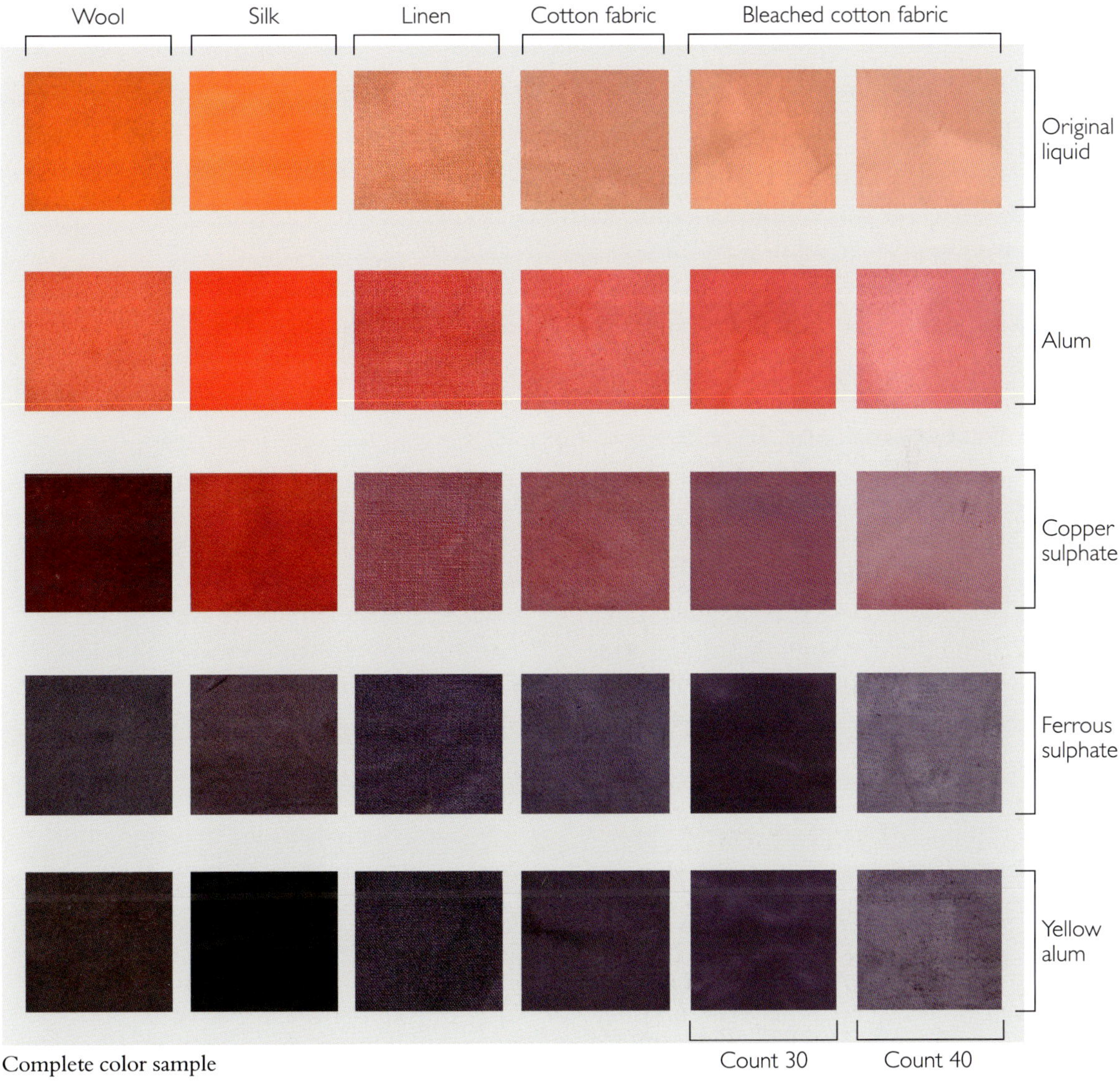

Wool
Silk
Linen
Cotton fabric
Bleached cotton fabric

Original liquid
Alum
Copper sulphate
Ferrous sulphate
Yellow alum

Count 30
Count 40

Complete color sample

2. Red Series: Safflower

Safflower is an annual or biennial herbaceous plant of the Asteraceae family, native to the Middle East. It was introduced to China during the Han dynasty by Zhang Qian and is now cultivated in regions such as Henan, Hunan, Sichuan, Xinjiang, and Xizang.

The flowers of the safflower contain two types of pigments, yellow and red. The yellow pigment, which is water and acid soluble, accounts for about 95% of the total pigment content. The red pigment, which is soluble in alkaline solutions, makes up about 5%. Both pigments can be used for dyeing. The yellow pigment dyes silk and wool in an orange hue, while it is more difficult to dye cotton and linen fabrics, resulting in a light yellow color. Overall, the colorfastness of the yellow pigment is relatively poor, and it is generally used less frequently for dyeing. The red pigment has a very low concentration, so much more is required compared to other plant dyes to achieve a rich red color.

Both fresh and dried safflower flowers can be used for dyeing. In ancient times, safflower was often made into safflower cakes for preservation. Safflower is also a traditional Chinese medicinal herb, known for its properties of promoting blood circulation, relieving blood stasis, and reducing pain. Safflower seeds can also be pressed to extract oil for consumption.

Dye Extraction and Effects

Step 1:

Mix 250 g of safflower with 3,000 ml of clean water and place the mixture in a pot. Let it sit for 12 hours. The yellow pigment in the safflower is water soluble, and after resting, it will be easier to extract the yellow pigment.

Step 2:

After resting, the water will turn yellow, indicating that some of the yellow pigment has dissolved into the water while some remains on the safflower. At this point, use gauze to filter the water. It is recommended to place the gauze on a fine mesh strainer for better filtration.

Step 3:

After filtering, wrap the safflower in gauze and repeatedly rub and squeeze it. Then, place the gauze bundle in clean water and continue to rinse and massage to release the remaining yellow pigment.

Step 4:

Repeat the rubbing and squeezing process 6 to 8 times as described in Step 3, until the yellow pigment is thoroughly washed out and the water runs clear. In the image, the safflower in the top bowl changes from an orange red color to a yellow brown hue after multiple washes. The three bowls at the bottom show the changes in the yellow pigment at different stages of the washing process.

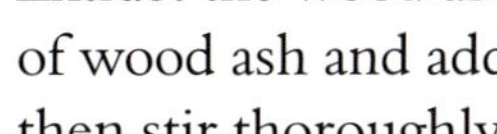

Step 5:

Extract the wood ash water. Take 300 g of wood ash and add 6,000 ml of water, then stir thoroughly. Let it sit for 48 hours. The alkali in the wood ash will gradually dissolve into the water.

Step 6:

During the resting period, the cloudy wood ash will slowly settle at the bottom, and the upper layer will become clear, resembling clean water. The rim of the container may have a small amount of wood ash residue, which is normal. Pour the clear wood ash water from the upper layer into another container. Test the pH of the solution using pH paper, which should show a value between 9 and 11.

7
8
9
10
11
12
13
14
15
16

Step 7:

Mix 3,000 ml of wood ash water with the washed safflower in a container. Let it sit for 24 hours. The red pigment in the safflower is soluble in the alkaline solution, and the red pigment will gradually precipitate out over time.

Step 8:

After resting for 24 hours, the wood ash water will change from clear to red. Continue to rub the safflower, allowing the remaining red pigment on the flowers to dissolve into the wood ash water.

Step 9:

Use a fine mesh sieve to filter the safflower, removing any remaining residues, to obtain 3,000 ml of dye liquid.

Step 10:

Place the safflower back into the container. Compared to the first soak, the safflower will change from a bright red to an orange red color. Add 3,000 ml of wood ash water for the second extraction and let it sit for 24 hours.

Step 11:

Repeat Steps 8 and 9 to extract the second batch of dye liquid. In the image, the left side shows the second extraction, and the right side shows the first extraction. There is a noticeable gradation of color from light to dark. Mix both dye liquids to complete the dye extraction.

Step 12:

Prepare the acid agent. Take 5 smoked plums and add 300 ml of water. Boil for 30 minutes. Smoked plums are a commonly used acid agent in traditional dyeing methods. You can also use other acid agents, such as vinegar, in which case Step 13 is not needed.

Step 13:

Strain out the plum juice. Add another 300 ml of water and boil for 30 minutes, then strain again. Combine both batches of plum juice.

Step 14:

Pour the plum juice or other acid agent into the extracted safflower dye liquid in small amounts, repeatedly adding until the pH test with pH paper shows a value of about 7.5, indicating that the acidity and alkalinity have been neutralized to a neutral state. The remaining plum juice can be stored for future use.

Step 15:

Divide the extracted 6,000 ml of dye liquid into five separate containers. Mix the mordants with the dye liquid, adding 3 to 5 g of mordant for every 1,200 ml of dye liquid. Stir continuously until the mordant is completely dissolved. Then, add the acid agent until the pH of the dye liquid reaches 6 when tested with pH paper. This dyeing process will involve extracting color samples using the original dye liquid and four different mordant solutions. From left to right, the color samples are: safflower original liquid, alum mordant solution, copper sulphate mordant solution, ferrous sulphate mordant solution, and yellow alum mordant solution.

Step 16:

Soak the cotton, linen, cashmere, and silk fabrics in water to dampen them, then place them into the dye liquid. Let them soak at room temperature for 2 to 4 hours, removing the fabrics one by one afterwards. During this process, the pH value should be measured multiple times. If the acidity decreases, add more acid agent to bring the pH value back to around 6. Throughout the process, the dye liquid should be stirred continuously to ensure that the fabrics absorb the dye evenly.

Step 17:

After mordanting, remove the fabric from the dye bath and rinse it until all excess color is removed. Gently wring out the water and hang the fabric to dry. Once it is half or completely dry, iron it to smooth out the fabric if necessary. The image shows the result of dyeing with safflower original liquid.

Step 18:

Organize and archive the dyed fabric samples and threads, recording the corresponding values and amounts used. During future dyeing projects, you can choose the appropriate fabric and mordant based on the color samples to guide artistic creation. The image shows the dyeing effect of safflower original liquid on different fabrics. The red pigment in safflower is highly sensitive to changes in acidity and alkalinity, and the pH variation during the dyeing process directly affects the color outcome.

Dye Color Samples

❖Red Pigment

Safflower original liquid

Safflower + alum

Safflower + copper sulphate

Safflower + ferrous sulphate

Safflower + yellow alum

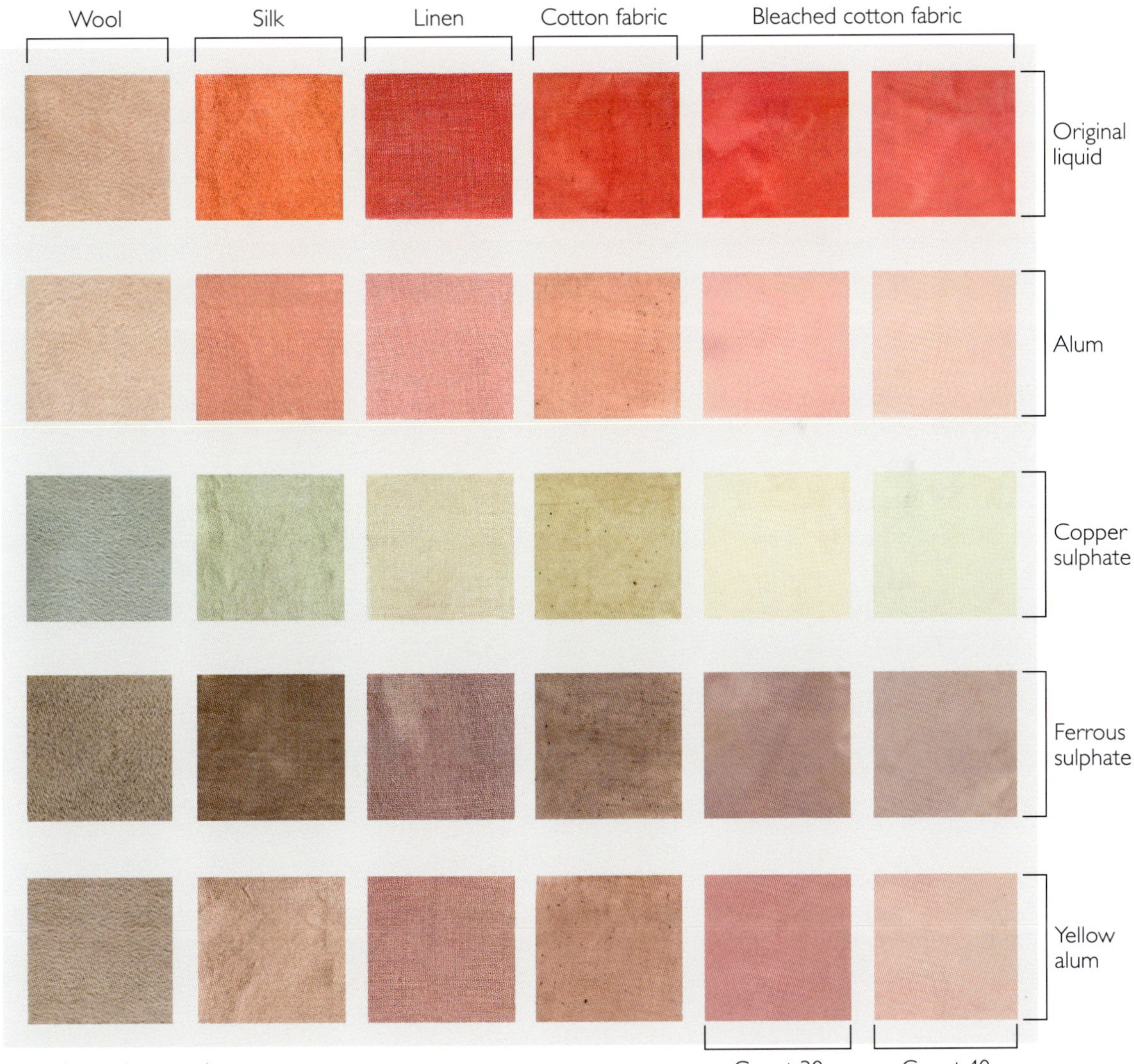

	Wool	Silk	Linen	Cotton fabric	Bleached cotton fabric (Count 30)	Bleached cotton fabric (Count 40)
Original liquid						
Alum						
Copper sulphate						
Ferrous sulphate						
Yellow alum						

Complete color sample

❖Yellow Pigment

The dye extracted in Steps 1 to 4 is the yellow pigment. As shown in the illustration, silk and wool absorb the color more effectively than cotton and linen, though the colorfastness is relatively poor. Creators may choose to use it according to their needs.

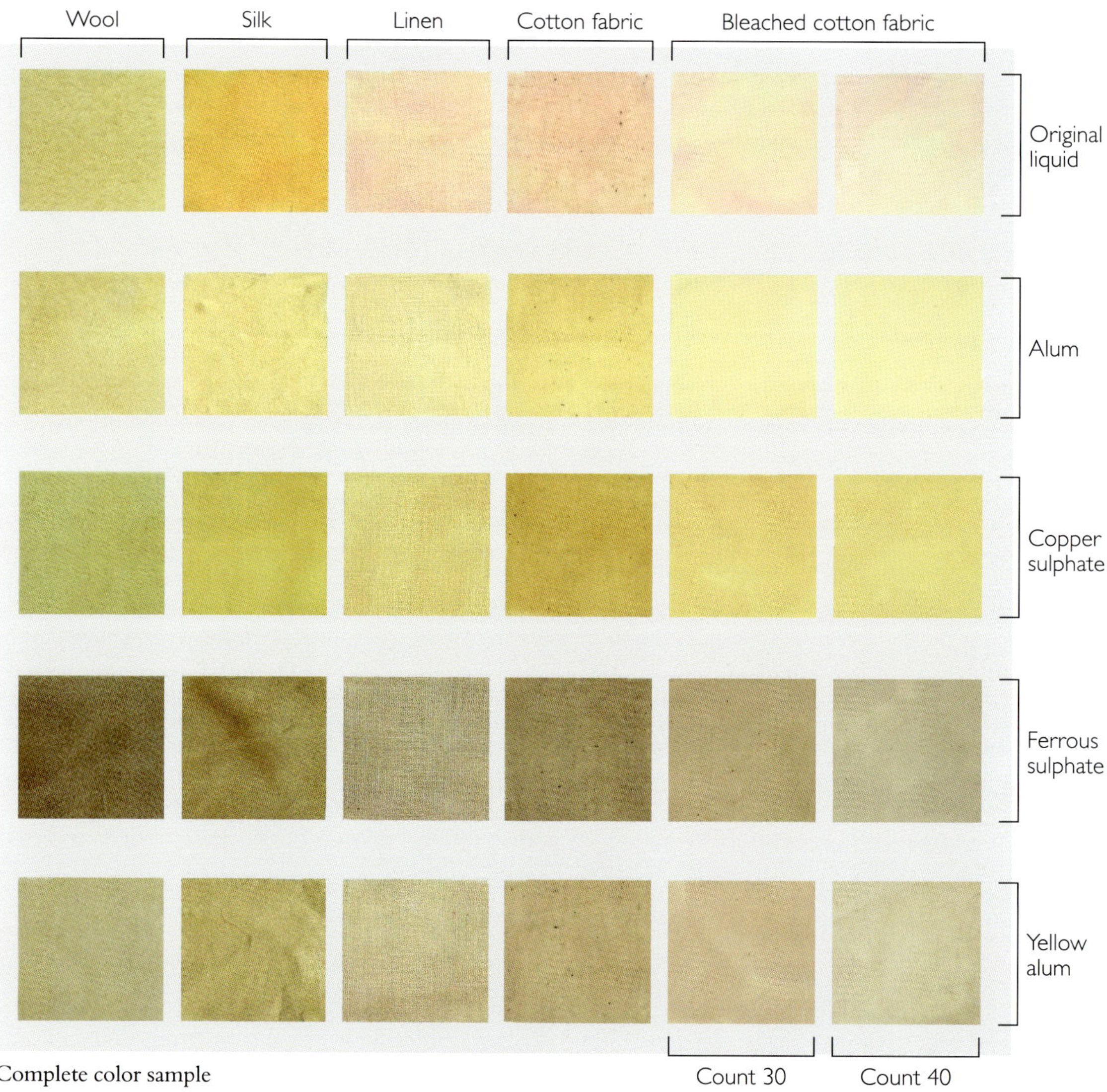

Complete color sample

3. Yellow Series: Gardenia

Gardenia, a genus of evergreen shrubs in the Rubiaceae family, is cultivated throughout south central and southwestern China. Its fruit contains gardenia yellow pigment and crocetin. The crocetin is the key pigment used to directly dye fabrics a bright and pure yellow. With the addition of mordants, it can also produce yellow green tones leaning towards olive yellow as well as ginger yellow. Gardenia was a highly important yellow dye in ancient China. However, the lightfastness of gardenia is relatively poor, not as good as that of amur cork tree and sophora flower. Gardenia fruit can be used in traditional medicine, possessing properties that clear heat, purge fire, cool the blood, and detoxify. As a natural colorant, it is also used in the food and cosmetics industries.

Dye Extraction and Effects

Step 1:

Mix 250 g of gardenia fruits with 2,500 ml of clean water in a pot. Bring to a boil over high heat, then simmer gently for 30 minutes to carry out the first extraction.

Step 2:

Filter the boiled mixture using a fine mesh sieve to remove the gardenia fruit residues and collect the dye liquid.

Step 3:

Return the filtered gardenia fruits to the pot and repeat Steps 1 and 2 for a second extraction. Combine both rounds of extracted dye liquid to yield approximately 5,000 ml of dye solution.

Step 4:

Divide the extracted 5,000 ml of dye liquid into five containers. Prepare the mordant mixtures by adding 3 to 5 g of mordant per 1,000 ml of dye liquid. After dissolving, pre-wet fabric swatches of different materials and sizes, then immerse them in the dye solutions for 2 to 4 hours. From left to right, the dyeing samples are gardenia original liquid, ferrous sulphate mordant solution, alum mordant solution, copper sulphate mordant solution, and yellow alum mordant solution.

1

2

3

4

Step 5:

After completing the mordanting process, remove the fabric from the dye bath and rinse thoroughly with water until all floating color is removed. The image shows the fabric sample dyed with gardenia original liquid.

Step 6:

Hang the dyed fabric samples to dry in batches. Organize and archive them properly. The image shown is the fabric sample dyed using gardenia original liquid.

Dye Color Samples

Gardenia original liquid

Gardenia + alum

Gardenia + copper sulphate

Gardenia + ferrous sulphate

Gardenia + yellow alum

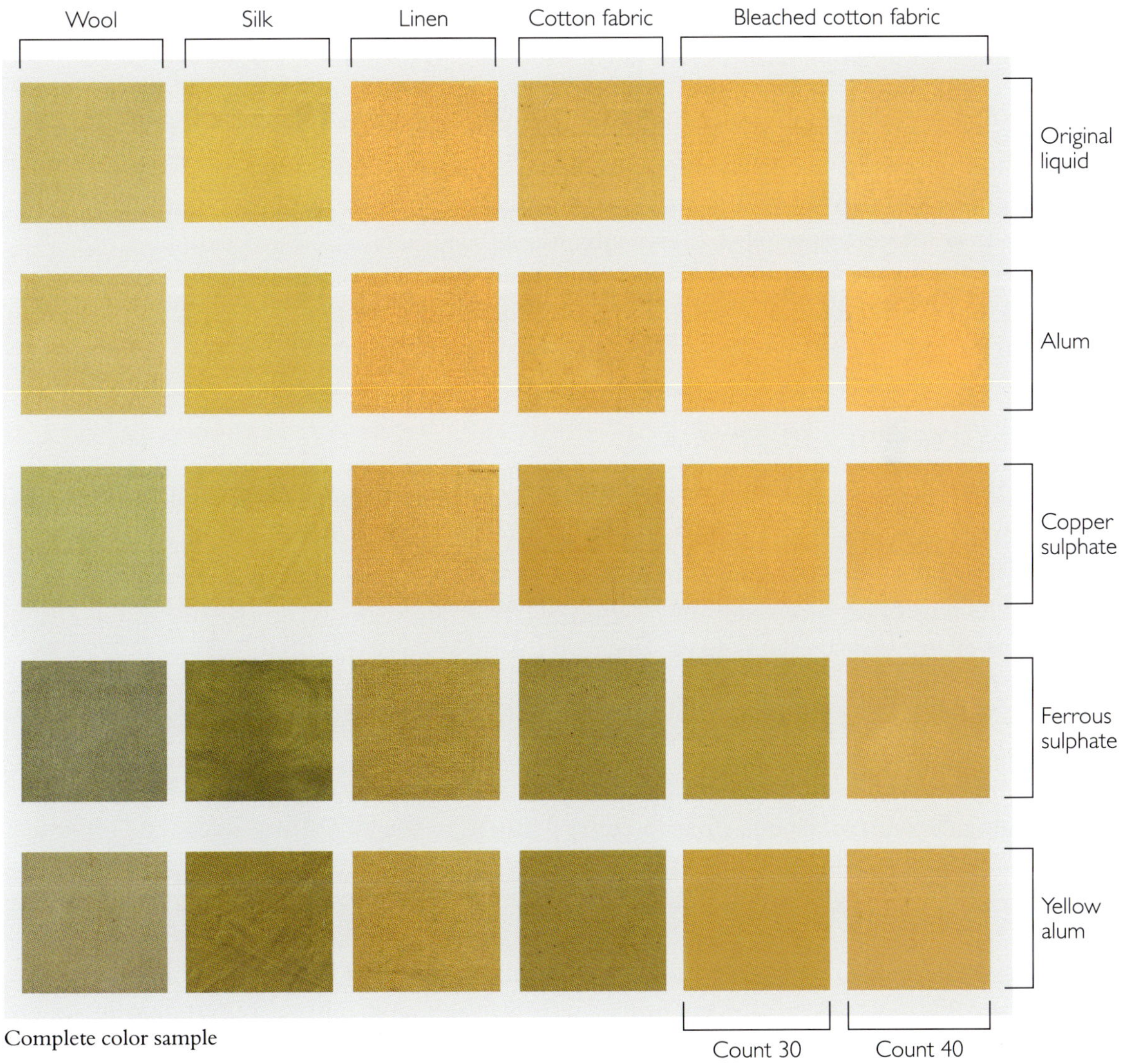

Wool

Silk

Linen

Cotton fabric

Bleached cotton fabric

Original liquid

Alum

Copper sulphate

Ferrous sulphate

Yellow alum

Count 30

Count 40

Complete color sample

4. Yellow Series: Amur Cork Tree

Amur cork tree, a deciduous tree of the Rutaceae family, is a medicinal tree species. It is widely distributed across northern and southern China and is also cultivated in Japan, Korea, Central Asia, and Eastern Europe. It has antibacterial, antihypertensive, bile-promoting, and cough-relieving properties.

Amur cork tree is an important plant for creating yellow dyes. The primary dyeing material is the bast. The outer surface of the bark is yellow brown, while the inner bark is a bright yellow. The bark is rich in berberine, which is the main pigment responsible for the yellow color. The resulting yellow dye is bright and vivid. Amur cork tree can be used to dye fabrics directly to produce a bright yellow color, or it can be combined with various mordants to produce other shades, such as olive green, medium green, or gray green.

In addition to its use in dyeing, berberine, the active compound in amur cork tree, also has insect repellent properties. In ancient China, not only was amur cork tree used to dye silk and fabric, but its insect repellent characteristic was also utilized for dyeing paper. This was particularly useful for documents that needed to be preserved for long periods, such as scriptures and account books.

Dye Extraction and Effects

Step 1:

Mix 250 g of amur cork tree with 2,500 ml of water in a pot. Bring it to a boil over high heat, then reduce the heat to a simmer and cook for 30 minutes to complete the first extraction.

Step 2:

Use a fine mesh sieve to filter the liquid, separating the amur cork tree from the dye extract.

Step 3:

Reintroduce the amur cork tree back into the pot and repeat the process from Step 1 and Step 2 for a second extraction. Combine the two batches of liquid to yield approximately 5,000 ml of dye extract.

Step 4:

Divide the 5,000 ml of extracted dye into 5 separate containers. Mix mordants with the dye by adding 3 to 5 g of mordant per 1,000 ml of dye liquid. After dissolving the mordant, moisten fabric samples and soak them in the dye solution for 2 to 4 hours. The dyeing samples, from left to right, are amur cork tree original liquid, ferrous sulphate mordant solution, alum mordant solution, copper sulphate mordant solution, and yellow alum mordant solution.

Step 5:

After the mordanting process, remove the fabric and wash it thoroughly until all excess color is removed. The image demonstrates the effect of dyeing with amur cork tree and alum.

Step 6:

Dry the fabric samples in batches, ensuring they are properly organized and archived. The image shows the fabric samples dyed with amur cork tree and alum.

Dye Color Samples

Amur cork tree original liquid

Amur cork tree + alum

Amur cork tree + copper sulphate

Amur cork tree + ferrous sulphate

Amur cork tree
+ yellow alum

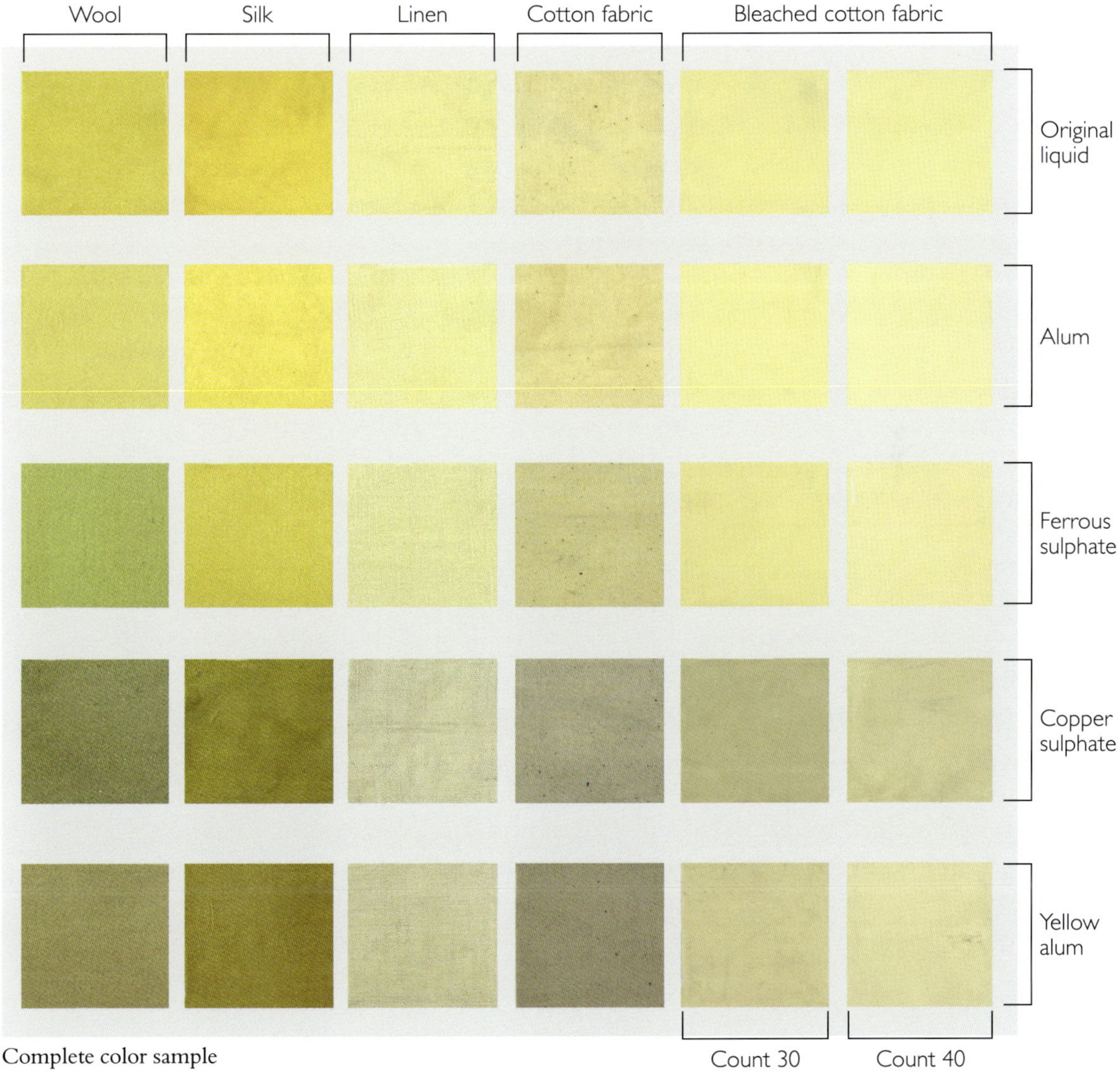

	Wool	Silk	Linen	Cotton fabric	Bleached cotton fabric	
					Count 30	Count 40
Original liquid						
Alum						
Ferrous sulphate						
Copper sulphate						
Yellow alum						

Complete color sample

5. Blue Series: Indigo Plants

Indigo plants is a general term for plants used for blue dyeing. They are rich in indigotin which is essential for traditional dyeing. The most commonly used indigo plants are four types, Chinese indigo, Chinese rain bell, woad, and true indigo.

In China, all four types of indigo plants are cultivated, with Chinese indigo being the most common. Studies show that the indigo content in these plants is highest in true indigo and lowest in woad. The wash fastness and light fastness of indigo dyed fabrics are superior to those of other plant dyes. Additionally, indigo dye can be extracted into solid indigo paste for long-term storage, unaffected by the seasonal limitations of plant cultivation and harvesting. As a result, it has become one of the most widely used plant dyes in China and globally. In addition, indigo plants have antibacterial, anti-inflammatory, and heat clearing properties, as well as detoxifying effects.

The extraction methods for indigo plants are divided into fresh leaf dyeing and indigo production dyeing. Fresh leaf dyeing involves chopping freshly harvested leaves and soaking them in water to extract the dye. This method works because the fresh leaves contain water-soluble blue pigment (original indigo pigment), which can be directly extracted to produce indigo dye. However, once the fresh leaves dry, the water soluble pigment transforms into the non-water-soluble indigo pigment, making it impossible to use this method for dyeing once the leaves are dried. Additionally, the pigment extracted using this method is limited and relatively small in quantity, making it suitable primarily for dyeing silk. Cotton and linen fabrics rarely absorb the dye, and the resulting color tends to be dark and dull.

Indigo production dyeing involves fermenting fresh leaves to create indigo mud, which is a reducing dye. The process involves mixing the indigo mud with water in the required amounts to create a dye bath for coloring. This method is the most conventional for indigo dyeing. Since indigo plants contain indole derivatives, these substances undergo oxidation to produce indigo, which then forms indigo mud. During the dyeing process, the indigo mud undergoes a reduction reaction, allowing the pigment to dissolve in water and bind to the fabric. Afterward, the fabric is exposed to air to oxidize and develop color. Different regions and types of indigo plants may use slightly different methods to produce indigo, such as in Japan, where a fermentation process using dry hay piles is employed to extract indigo mud.

Dye Extraction and Effects

For this operation, the plant used is the Chinese indigo from Sichuan, China, and the indigo is produced by the fresh leaf precipitation fermentation method.

Step 1:

Take 2.5 kg fresh indigo plant and place it in a suitably sized container. During production, the choice of local and seasonal indigo plants can be made according to personal circumstances. The indigo plant must be freshly picked and used. It cannot be stored for extended periods.

Step 2:

Add clean water to immerse the indigo plant. The water level should completely submerge the indigo plant. Heavy objects can be placed on top of the plant to press it down and prevent parts from floating to the surface, which could lead to incomplete extraction of the dye.

Step 3:

Soak the indigo plant in water for 2 to 3 days. During this process, the plant will change color from green to brown. When the leaves have fully turned brown, this step is complete. At this point, the indole derivatives in the plant will be released and dissolved in the water, turning the water green and forming a small amount of blue oxidation film on the surface. It is normal for the fermentation process to produce a plant-like rotten odor.

Step 4:

Once soaking is complete, remove all the indigo plant. The grass is no longer useful and can be disposed of as fertilizer. At this point, the liquid in the container will be a deep green color, with the upper layer appearing light green.

Siphon Method

The siphon method is a technique that uses the liquid's own gravity and the difference in atmospheric pressure to transfer liquid. The core principle is based on atmospheric pressure and the force of gravity acting on the liquid. When a pipe connects two liquid surfaces at different heights, the pressure at the higher liquid level is greater than that at the lower level. Under this pressure difference, the liquid flows from the higher level to the lower level. In addition, gravity helps the liquid to continue flowing through the pipe.

Operating Steps:

1. Prepare a flexible hose, ensuring it is long enough to connect the two containers.
2. Place one end of the hose into the higher container, making sure it is fully submerged in the liquid. Use your finger to seal the other end to prevent air from entering.
3. Move the sealed end into the lower container, ensuring that the outlet is positioned below the liquid level of the higher container.
4. Release your finger – at this point, the liquid will begin to flow naturally.

Step 5:

Prepare a stick and 40 g of quicklime powder, which should be about 3% of the total weight of the indigo plant. Add the quicklime powder to the liquid obtained in the previous step and immediately begin vigorously striking the surface of the water with the stick (5-a). This step is called "beating the indigo," and its purpose is to oxidize the water soluble indole derivatives into insoluble indigo, which then combines with calcium ions from the quicklime to slowly form a precipitate. Continue beating the liquid for 30 minutes. In the early stages, the dye liquid will turn yellow green, and a large amount of light blue foam will appear (5-b). In the middle stages, the dye liquid will change from yellow green to gray green, and a large amount of dark blue foam will form (5-c). When the surface foam turns from dark blue to white (5-d) and quickly disappears, accompanied by a swishing sound as the foam disappears, the beating process is complete.

Step 6:

After completing the indigo beating, allow the dye liquid to stand for 12 hours. The indigo will fully precipitate at the bottom of the container, and the upper layer will be a semi-transparent tea brown liquid (6-a), which is indigo brown. This liquid needs to be drained. Use a soft hose siphon method (6-b) to draw off the tea brown liquid and extract the indigo at the bottom. It is not recommended to use a spoon or similar container to remove the liquid, as the indigo at the bottom has not fully solidified, and the spoon's contact with the surface may cause the indigo to float back into the water.

Step 7:

After completely siphoning off the tea brown liquid, pour the indigo paste into a container and allow it to continue draining excess water. This completes the extraction of indigo.

Step 8:

Prepare the indigo paste, alkali and reducing agent. Here's 50 g of indigo paste. You can use about 1 g of either quicklime powder or food grade soda ash as the alkali agent. For a traditional method, use a reducing agent such as glucose, white liquor, or rice wine. Both liquors contain glucose and can trigger a reduction reaction. If using glucose, 15 to 20 g will be sufficient. If using white liquor or rice wine, 100 ml will be sufficient. Alternatively, a commercially available strong reducing agent can be used, but since these are chemical products, a mask should be worn during use. A strong reducing agent usually requires only about 1 g, and 500 ml of clean water.

Step 9:
Dissolve the alkali in a small amount of warm water, then mix it with the indigo paste. Add 500 ml of clean water and stir thoroughly to ensure the indigo paste is fully diluted. Then add glucose, white liquor, or another reducing agent.

Step 10:
Let the solution sit for a period of time. Observe the dye liquid change from blue to bluish green. This indicates it's ready for dyeing. The traditional reduction process is relatively gentle and takes longer. Depending on the climate, it may require 2 to 3 days. Using a strong reducing agent shortens the process to about 20 to 30 minutes before dyeing can begin.

Step 11:
Immerse the fabric in the dye solution for approximately 10 to 20 minutes, then remove it. Upon removal, the fabric will appear fluorescent green. As it comes into contact with air, it will gradually oxidize and turn blue. The immersion time can be adjusted based on the creator's preference and the specific indigo extract used.

Step 12:
Once the fabric has fully turned blue, return it to the dye bath and repeat Step 11. Repeat this cycle as needed. The more times the fabric is dyed, the deeper the resulting color. The image shows the color of the wet fabric after two (12-a) and six (12-b) dyeing cycles.

9

10

11

12-a

12-b

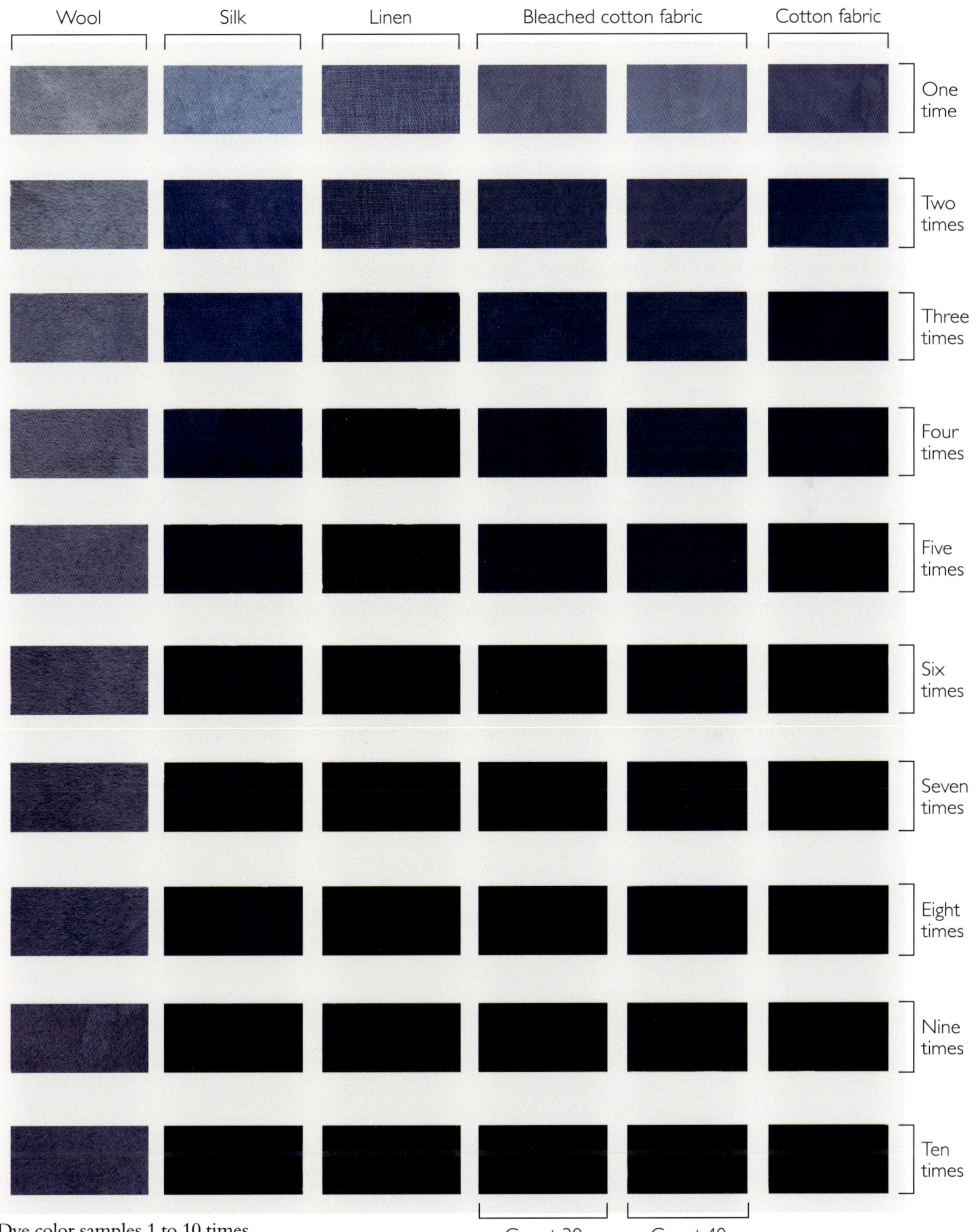

Dye color samples 1 to 10 times.

Key Points

1. Regarding the timing of indigo dye usage: During the dyeing process, the indigo dye will gradually oxidize from a greenish-blue color to the original blue color seen after the indigo paste dissolves. Once it has fully oxidized into blue, even if fabric is immersed in the dye bath, it will no longer absorb color. At this stage, it is necessary to add more reducing agent to convert the dye back into its greenish blue reduced state. Only then can the dyeing process continue effectively. If the dye bath turns from greenish-blue to dark green during the dyeing process, it indicates that oxidation has begun. While dyeing is still possible at this stage, the color uptake will be less effective. The best dyeing results occur when the dye bath is clearly greenish blue in color. The time it takes for the dye to oxidize from greenish-blue to blue is not fixed. It can be influenced by factors such as the frequency of use, the amount of fabric dyed, and the specific dyeing methods employed. To slow down oxidation, it's advisable to cover the dye bath with a lid during use. Alternatively, increasing the volume of the dye solution can help. For instance, a 10 liter dye bath oxidizes more slowly than a 5 liter one.
2. The recommended ratio of indigo paste to water is 100 g of indigo paste to 1,000 ml of water. If the fabric is large and cannot be fully submerged during the dyeing process, you may add more water until the fabric is completely covered. However, note that adding water will dilute the dye concentration.
3. As the dyeing process continues and more fabric absorbs color, the amount of indigo in the dye bath will gradually decrease. In this case, you can prepare a fresh batch of dye solution and combine it with the existing dye bath for continued use.
4. Regarding the ratios of alkaline agents, glucose, and liquor used during indigo extraction and dyeing, it is difficult to provide a one-size-fits-all formula due to variations in indigo plant species and differences in the concentration of lime powder and alcohol. Creators are encouraged to make slight adjustments based on the guidelines provided in this book.
5. If indigo paste is commercially available, it can be purchased directly and used for dyeing without the need for extraction.

Color samples dyed with indigo after different immersion times.

6. Purple Series: Purple Gromwell

Gromwell is a perennial herbaceous plant from the Boraginaceae family, primarily produced in China. It was an important plant for dyeing purple in ancient times, widely used in the clothing of royalty and officials. During the Spring and Autumn period (770–476 BC), Duke Huan of Qi favored purple, making it a national trend. As a result, purple garments became symbols of high status and distinction. The roots of purple gromwell contain a high concentration of purple pigment called shikonin, which can be used for dyeing. However, shikonin is not easily soluble in water, but dissolves well in alcohol, oil, and wax, so alcohol is commonly used to extract the dye.

There are two main types of gromwell, soft gromwell and hard gromwell. Soft gromwell typically refers to varieties produced in Xinjiang and Gansu of China. These have relatively soft roots and a higher shikonin content, yielding vivid purple hues. Hard gromwell is mainly found in northeastern

Cotton threads dyed with purple gromwell using different mordants.

and northern China, with harder roots that tend to produce brownish gray tones. In addition to its use in dyeing, gromwell is also a traditional medicinal herb, known for its anti-inflammatory, antibacterial, and antidepressant properties.

Dye Extraction and Effects

Step 1:

Prepare 250 g of purple gromwell, 5 L of alcohol (75% medical ethanol is recommended to reduce fire risk), and a sealed container with a capacity greater than 2.5 L.

Step 2:

Place the gromwell into the container and pour in 2,500 ml of alcohol. Seal the container tightly and let it sit for 24 hours.

Step 3:

Use a strainer or filter to separate the gromwell from the liquid, yielding approximately 2,500 ml of dye solution.

Step 4:

Proceed with a second extraction. Reuse the filtered gromwell and repeat Steps 2 and 3. This will result in a total of 5,000 ml of dye solution.

Step 5:

Divide the 5,000 ml of dye solution into 5 separate containers. Then, add the mordant to each container. For every 1,000 ml of dye solution, add 3 to 5 g of mordant. Stir the dye solution continuously to ensure the mordant is fully dissolved. As a result, the dye solution will display different colors. In this dyeing process, the original dye solution is mixed with four types of mordant solutions to create color samples. From left to right, the samples are gromwell original liquid, alum mordant solution, copper sulphate mordant solution, ferrous sulphate mordant solution, and yellow alum mordant solution.

Step 6:

Soak the cotton, linen, cashmere, and silk fabrics in water to dampen them. Then, place the fabrics into the dye solution. Let them soak at room temperature for 2 to 4 hours, and take them out one by one afterwards. During the process, make sure to stir the dye solution continuously to ensure the fabrics absorb the dye evenly.

Step 7:

After the mordanting process is complete, remove the fabrics from the dye solution and rinse them with water until the excess dye is completely removed. Gently wring out the fabric and hang it to dry. Once the fabric is half or fully dried, you can iron it flat if necessary. The image shows the effect of soft gromwell original liquid with alum mordant.

Step 8:

Organize and archive the dyed fabric samples and threads, documenting the corresponding values and amounts used. During the dyeing process, you can choose the appropriate fabric and mordant based on the color samples for artistic creation. The image shows the effect of soft gromwell original liquid with alum mordant.

1

2

3

4

5

6

7

8

Dye Color Samples

❖Soft Gromwell

Gromwell original liquid

Gromwell + alum

Gromwell + copper sulphate

Gromwell + ferrous sulphate

Gromwell + yellow alum

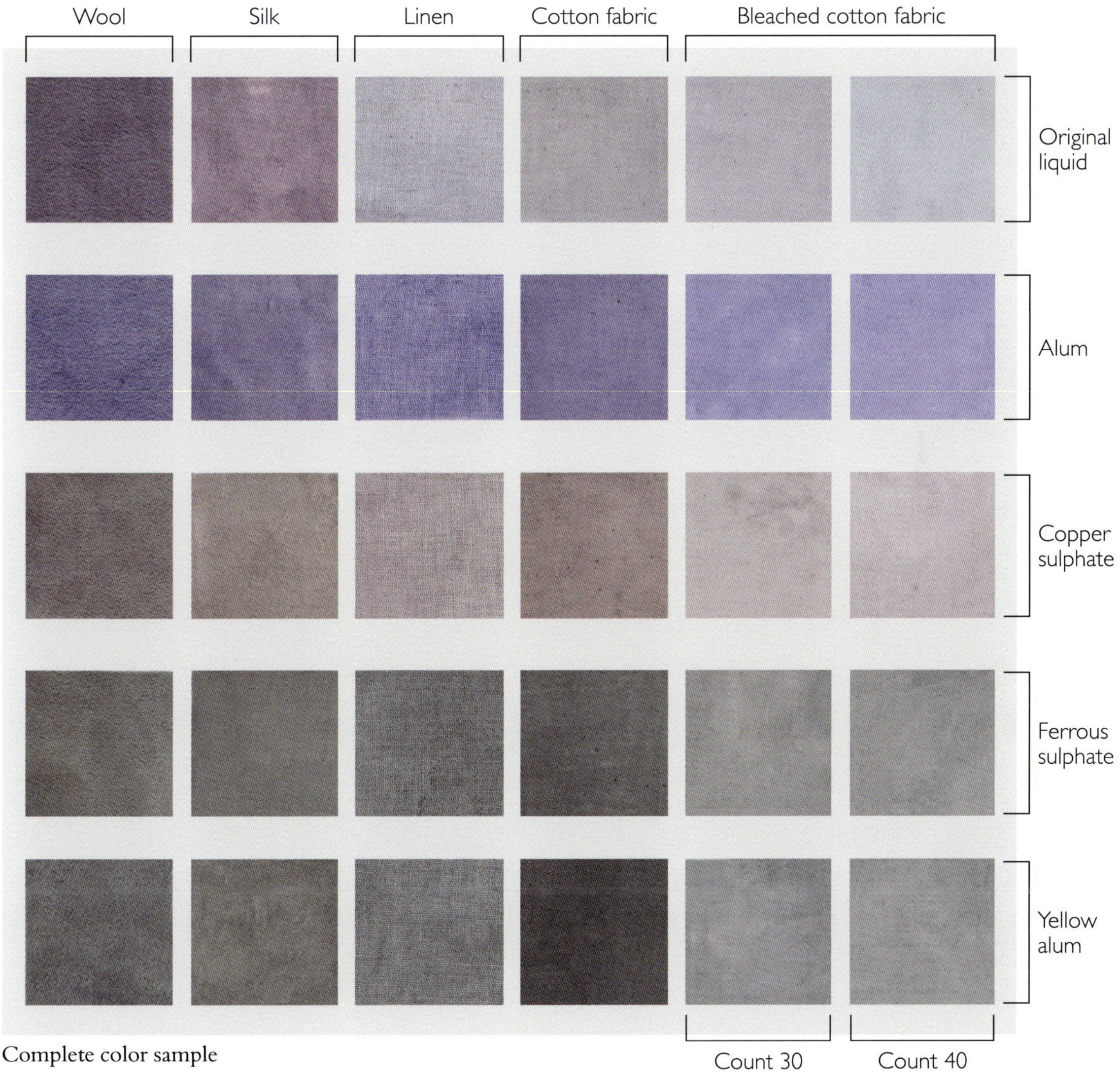

Wool
Silk
Linen
Cotton fabric
Bleached cotton fabric

Original liquid
Alum
Copper sulphate
Ferrous sulphate
Yellow alum

Count 30
Count 40

Complete color sample

❖Hard Gromwell

Gromwell original liquid

Gromwell + alum

Gromwell + copper sulphate

Gromwell + ferrous sulphate

Gromwell + yellow alum

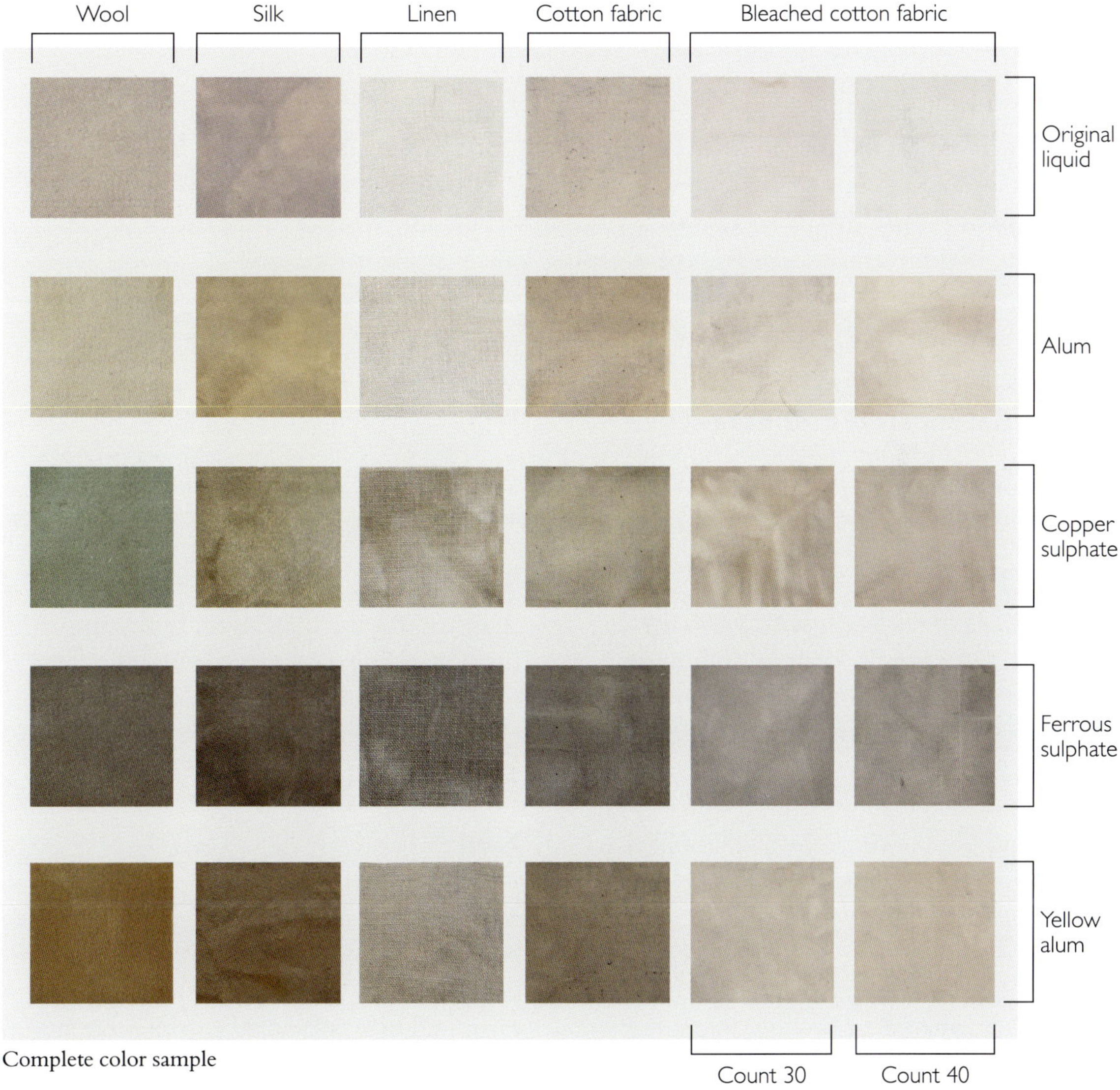

	Wool	Silk	Linen	Cotton fabric	Bleached cotton fabric	
					Count 30	Count 40
Original liquid						
Alum						
Copper sulphate						
Ferrous sulphate						
Yellow alum						

Complete color sample

7. Brown Series: Tea Leaves

Tea leaves belong to the Camellia genus in the Theaceae family. The tea tree is an evergreen shrub or small tree and is an important economic crop. China is the earliest country to have discovered and utilized the tea tree. Until today, tea is almost universally consumed in China, and it has also developed a rich tea culture and tea drinking customs, which have spread overseas, having a wide influence.

The tender leaves of the tea tree are the primary raw material for tea production. By controlling the degree of fermentation, different types of tea are processed, such as non-fermented green tea, semi-fermented oolong tea, fully fermented black tea, and post-fermented dark tea, among others. Tea leaves contain tea polyphenols, which, after oxidation, form the pigments thearubigins, theaflavins, and theabrownins. These three pigments can be used for dyeing, resulting in shades primarily of brownish gray. Tea polyphenols also have strong antioxidant properties and are beneficial for cardiovascular health, cancer prevention, and anti-inflammatory effects. Fabrics dyed with tea also exhibit excellent antibacterial properties.

Dye Extraction and Effects

For this operation, the choice is Zhengshan Xiaozhong black tea from Fujian Province, China, though the creator can also use any available black tea at home.

Step 1:
Mix 250 g of tea leaves with 3,000 ml of water in a pot. Bring it to a boil over high heat, then simmer for 30 minutes to perform the first extraction. Due to the evaporation of steam during the boiling process and the absorption of water by the tea leaves, approximately 2,500 ml of dye liquid will be obtained.

Step 2:
Use a fine mesh sieve to filter the dye liquid obtained after boiling, removing any tea leaf residue.

Step 3:
Reintroduce the filtered tea leaves into the pot and repeat Steps 1 and 2 to perform the second extraction. Combine the two batches of dye liquid, yielding approximately 5,000 ml of dye liquid.

Step 4:
Divide the extracted 5,000 ml of dye liquid into 5 separate containers and add 3 to 5 g of mordant to each 1,000 ml of dye liquid. After dissolving, wet the sample fabric and soak it in the dye liquid for 2 to 4 hours. The dyeing process is

as follows from left to right: original tea leaves liquid, ferrous sulphate mordant liquid, alum mordant liquid, copper sulphate mordant liquid, and yellow alum mordant liquid.

Step 5:

After mordanting, remove the fabric and wash it thoroughly until the excess color is completely removed. The image shows the effect of tea dyed with alum mordant liquid.

Step 6:

Dry the fabric samples in batches and organize them for archiving. The image shows the fabric sample dyed with tea and alum mordant liquid.

1

2

3

4

5

6

Dye Color Samples

Tea leaves original liquid

Tea leaves + alum

Tea leaves + copper sulphate

Tea leaves + ferrous sulphate

Tea leaves + yellow alum

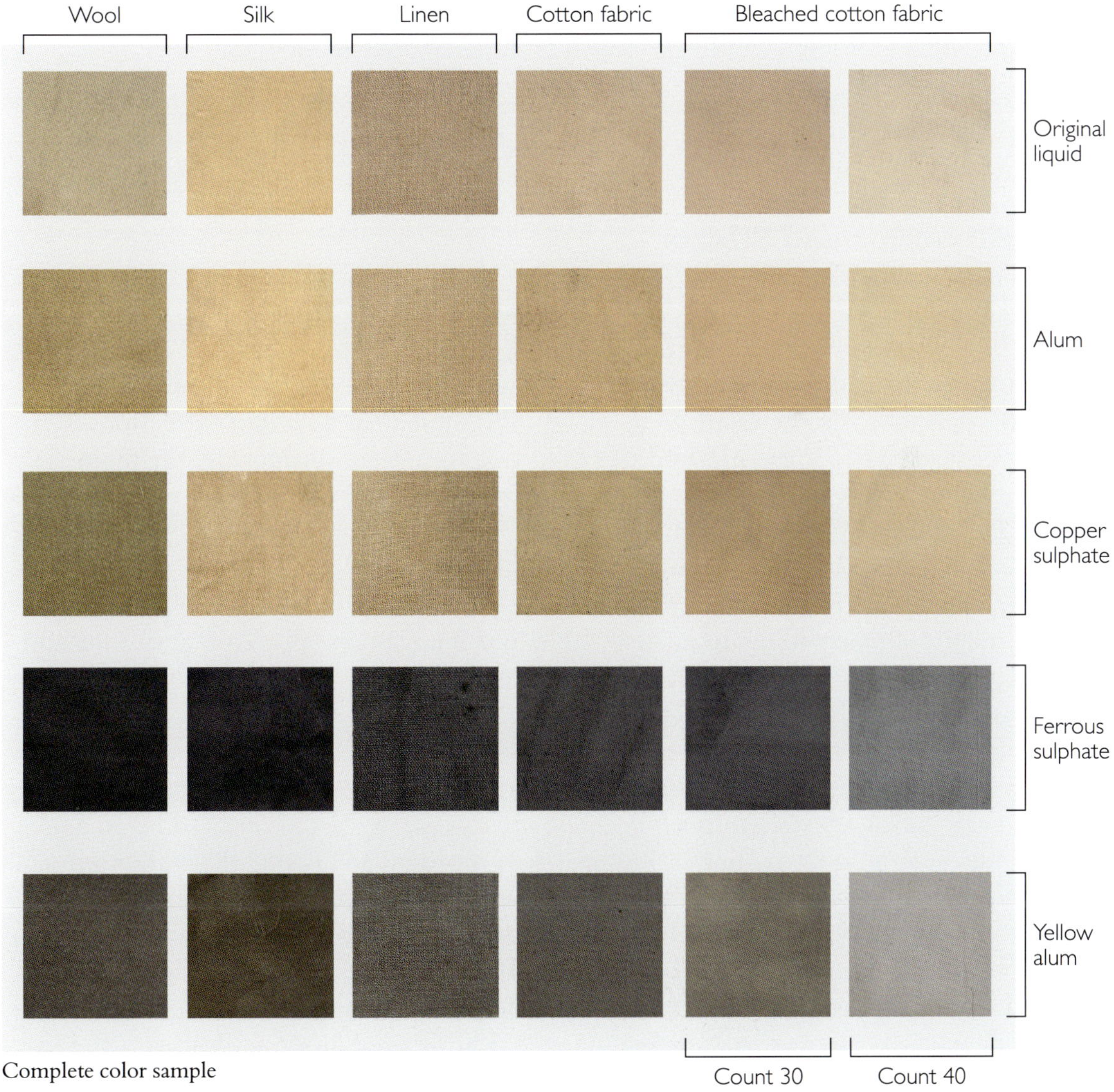

Wool Silk Linen Cotton fabric Bleached cotton fabric

Original liquid

Alum

Copper sulphate

Ferrous sulphate

Yellow alum

Count 30 Count 40

Complete color sample

8. Black Series: Betel Nut

Betel nut comes from a plant belonging to the palm family, which is an evergreen commonly found in Southern China, India, and Southeast Asia. It is an economic crop. The fruit contains arecoline, which, when processed and chewed, offers a taste that is initially bitter, followed by a sweet aftertaste. Due to this, it is also produced as a type of leisure food. However, prolonged consumption carries a high risk of cancer.

Betel nut contains tannic acid, which is a key substance for achieving black, gray, and brown tones in dyeing. Once the fruit ripens, it can be used as a dye. To extract the dye, the betel nut must be sliced or crushed and then steamed to better release the pigments. Additionally, when extracting the dye, it is necessary to add wood ash to help dissolve the tannic acid more effectively, which leads to a better dyeing result. Without this addition, the resulting color tone may be lighter.

Dye Extraction and Effects

Step 1:

Mix 250 g of betel nut slices with 3,000 ml of water in a pot, add wood ash water and stir well to make the solution's pH level reach 11 (for the method of making wood ash water, refer to Steps 5 and 6 on page 51). Bring the mixture to a boil over high heat, then simmer on low heat for 30 minutes, stirring the betel nut slices many times to ensure the pigment is fully extracted into the water. This is the first extraction. During this process, ensure the pot is tightly covered to prevent excessive water evaporation. After simmering, the dye solution should be around 2,500 ml due to evaporation.

Step 2:

Filter the betel nut using a fine mesh sieve, and a spoon can be used to assist in the process.

Step 3:

Return the filtered betel nut to the pot, add wood ash water, and repeat Step 1 and Step 2 for a second extraction. After two rounds of simmering, the pigment from the betel nut will be fully extracted.

Step 4:

Combine the dye extracts from Steps 2 and 3 to obtain approximately 5,000 ml of dye liquid.

Step 5:

Pour the 5,000 ml of extracted dye into five separate containers. Add 3 to 5 g of mordant to every 1,000 ml of dye liquid, stirring continuously to ensure the mordant is fully dissolved. The dye liquid will then display different colors. For this dyeing process, the original dye liquid is used along with four different mordants for color sample extraction,

with each mordant corresponding to a specific dye liquid.

Step 6:
Wet the cotton, linen, cashmere, or silk fabrics, then immerse them in the dye liquid. Allow the fabrics to soak at room temperature for 2 to 4 hours, stirring the dye periodically to ensure the fabric absorbs the dye evenly.

Step 7:
After mordanting, remove the fabric and wash it in water until the excess dye is completely rinsed off. Gently wring out any excess water and hang the fabric to dry. Once it is partially or fully dry, you can iron it to smooth it out as needed.

Step 8:
Organize and archive the dyed fabric samples and threads, recording the corresponding values and quantities. During the dyeing process, you can select suitable fabrics and mordants based on the color samples for artistic creation. To achieve a deeper brown black color, you can repeat the dyeing process multiple times, or combine different dyes. For example, you can first dye the fabric red or blue, then immerse it in the betel nut dye liquid to deepen the black color.

Dye Color Sample

Betel nut original liquid

Betel nut + alum

Betel nut + copper sulphate

Betel nut + ferrous sulphate

Betel nut + yellow alum

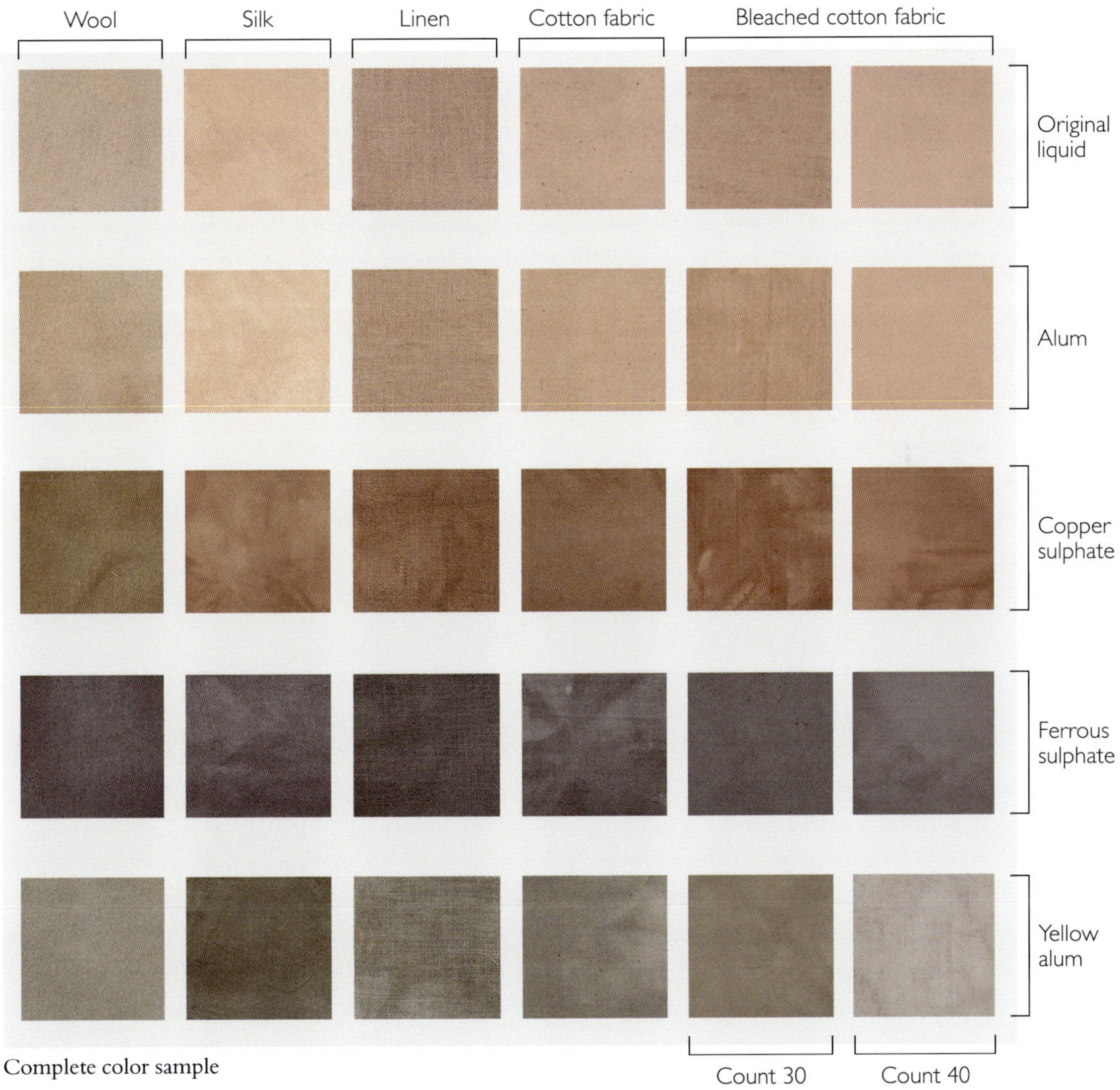

Wool
Silk
Linen
Cotton fabric
Bleached cotton fabric

Original liquid
Alum
Copper sulphate
Ferrous sulphate
Yellow alum

Count 30
Count 40

Complete color sample

9. Black Series: Chinese Nutgall

The Chinese nutgall is a product formed through the interaction of both animals and plants. It is a gall produced by the Chinese sumac aphid, which parasitizes on the branches of trees in the sumac family, such as the Chinese sumac, the Chinese varnish tree, and the Chinese gall. The Chinese nutgall forms when the plant is stimulated by the parasitic aphid, causing cell division and differentiation, resulting in a deformed tumor like growth. It also serves as the dwelling for the aphid. The outer shell is hard and thick, and the aphid's irregular movements inside lead to the gall expanding in various directions, resulting in various shapes.

Typically, Chinese nutgalls are harvested during the autumn equinox, when the pigment content is highest. After harvesting, it is necessary to first eliminate the aphids and then dry and store the gall. Chinese nutgalls contain abundant tannic acid, and when extracting the dye, it is important to add wood ash at the same time, or the resulting color will be lighter, presenting a khaki tone. In ancient times, in addition to dyeing fabrics, Chinese nutgalls were also used for dyeing hair. Chinese nutgalls are also a traditional medicinal herb, known for their hemostatic and antibacterial properties.

Dye Extraction and Effects

Step 1:

Mix 250 g of galls with 3,000 ml of water, and add wood ash water, stirring well to adjust the pH of the solution to 11. For the method of preparing wood ash water, refer to Steps 5 and 6 on page 51. Place the mixture in a pot and simmer for 30 minutes for the first extraction. Due to evaporation of water vapor during boiling and the plant's absorption of liquid, approximately 2,500 ml of dye solution is obtained.

Step 2:

Filter the dye solution obtained from boiling using a fine mesh strainer.

Step 3:

Refill the filtered galls into the pot, add wood ash water, and repeat Steps 1 and 2 for the second extraction. Combine both dye solutions to obtain approximately 5,000 ml of dye solution.

Step 4:

Pour the extracted 5,000 ml of dye solution into 5 separate measuring cylinders. Add 3 to 5 g of mordant to every 1,000 ml of dye solution. When the mordant has dissolved, dampen the fabric samples and immerse them in the dye solution for 2 to 4 hours. The dyeing process, from left to right, is as follows: nutgall original liquid, alum mordant solution, copper sulphate mordant solution, ferrous sulphate mordant solution, and yellow alum mordant solution.

Step 5:

After mordanting, remove the fabric and wash it until all excess color is removed. The image shows the result of using nutgall and ferrous sulphate mordant solution.

Step 6:

Dry the fabric samples in batches and organize them for archiving. The image shows the fabric sample dyed with nutgall and ferrous sulphate mordant solution. Since the color samples were dyed with a single 2 to 4 hour immersion, to achieve a deeper brown black color, multiple dips can be done using the ferrous sulphate or yellow alum mordant solutions. Alternatively, the fabric can be dyed red or blue first and then immersed in the nutgall dye solution to intensify the color.

Dye Color Samples

Chinese nutgall original liquid

Chinese nutgall + alum

Chinese nutgall + copper sulphate

Chinese nutgall + ferrous sulphate

Chinese nutgall + yellow alum

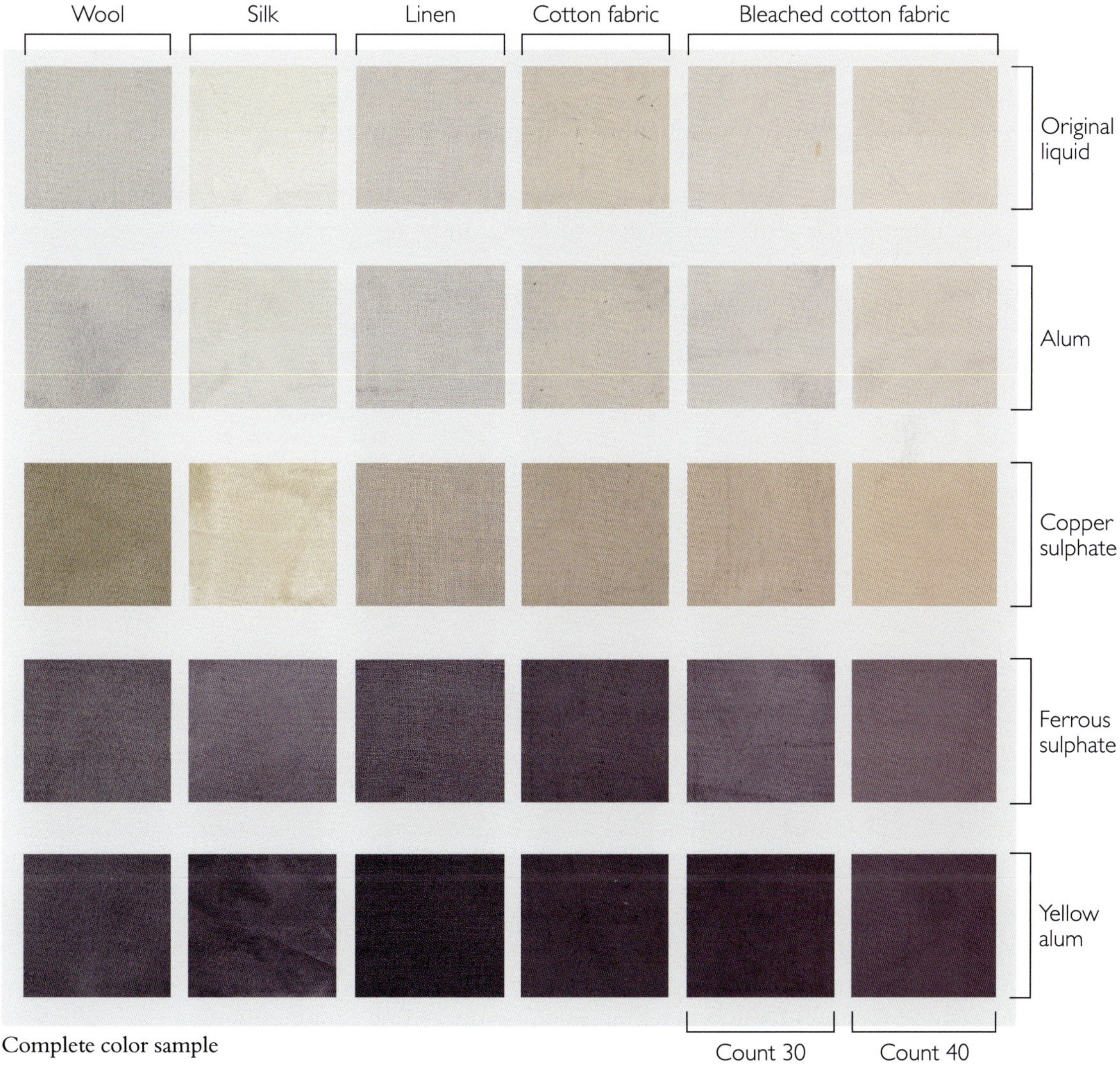

Wool
Silk
Linen
Cotton fabric
Bleached cotton fabric

Original liquid
Alum
Copper sulphate
Ferrous sulphate
Yellow alum

Count 30
Count 40

Complete color sample

Key Points of the Chapter

1. There are two methods for adding mordants in dyeing. The first method, as demonstrated in this chapter, involves directly mixing the mordant with the dye for dyeing. This method is more convenient. The second method involves dissolving the mordant in water, using 30 to 50 g of mordant for every liter of water. The fabric is first immersed in the mordant solution for 30 minutes, then removed and placed into the dye solution for another 30 minutes. This process is repeated 4 to 8 times until the desired color is achieved. This method is slower than the first but allows for better absorption of the dye. For lighter colors, either method can be used. However, for darker colors, it is recommended to use the second method.
2. Regarding the amount of dye material and water, when extracting dye liquid, the ratio of water to plant material does not need to be highly precise. Even with accurate measurements, color variations may still occur due to factors such as differences in plant batches or origin, which is an uncontrollable aspect of plant dyeing. Generally, the water should be enough to cover the plant material during the extraction process. Some plants absorb more water, so the amount of water can be increased accordingly. Less water will result in a more concentrated dye, while more water will dilute the pigment. When dyeing, fabrics tend to show darker colors when wet. Since it is difficult to observe the color directly, you can use a hair dryer to partially dry the fabric. If the desired color has not been reached, the fabric can be placed back in the dye solution for further soaking. Plant dyeing requires creators to gain experience through hands-on practice in order to handle the process with confidence and precision.
3. The color samples primarily serve as a reference for the creator. There are many factors that influence plant dyeing, and some plants are very sensitive to the pH level of the water. Creators should not become overly concerned or frustrated as this is an unavoidable uncertainty in plant dyeing. Additionally, the color samples in this chapter, except for the indigo-dyed ones, were dyed only once. Multiple dyeing sessions can deepen the color, and creators can build their own color sample library based on this.

On the facing page
Nutgall and color samples dyed with it using various mordants.

On the right
Stencil-dyed work featuring a circular floral motif.

CHAPTER FOUR

Applications of Plant Dyeing

When the colors of plants awaken on fabric, traditional dyeing techniques begin a dialogue with modern life. Centered around the theme "Function is Beauty," this chapter showcases a variety of works that transform botanical hues into practical aesthetics for daily living. By applying plant based dyes to diverse everyday items, such as scarves, bags, clothing, and home goods like curtains, we're able to find diverse carriers for plant dyeing. This chapter offers readers inspiration and creative ideas for using natural dyes. When we learn to adorn life with the colors of nature, we come to understand how to preserve the warmth of our palms and the breath of the seasons in an age of mechanical reproduction.

A batik work featuring plant motifs, dyed with sappanwood.

On the facing page
Impressions of Su Garden, a batik work made with cotton and organza patchwork.

1. Kerchief: *Geometric Rhythm*

This series of kerchiefs represents an introductory exploration of plant dyeing using tie dye techniques. Each of the three kerchiefs features a unique folding method, based on triangles, squares, and radiating circles, which serves as the foundation for the pattern design and tie dyeing process. By using structured geometric shapes, these designs create patterns that are both simple and rhythmically elegant, showcasing the unique charm of tie dye craftsmanship. These kerchiefs are not only suitable for everyday use but can also be hung as decorative pieces, adding a touch of beauty and warmth to any living space.

❖Kerchief A

Material Preparation

1. One silk kerchief. This piece uses a 12 momme pure white silk crepe satin, measuring 54 × 54 cm.
2. Two right angled triangular wooden boards, with the perpendicular sides longer than 8 cm.
3. One G-clamp, capable of clamping fabric thicker than 1.5 cm.
4. Two medium sized binder clips, capable of clamping fabric thicker than 1.5 cm.
5. Dye plant: Amur cork tree.
6. Mordant: Ferrous sulphate.

Steps

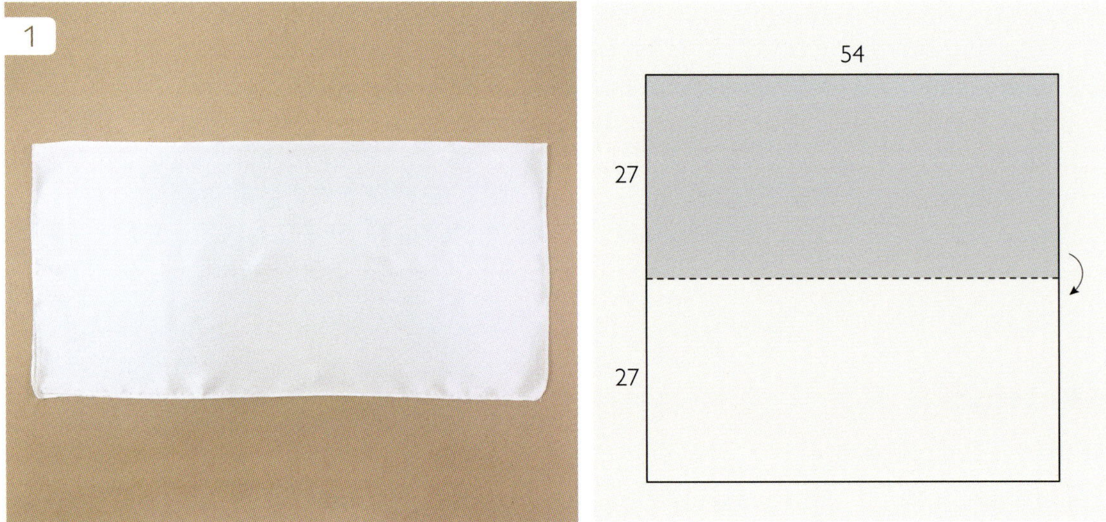

Open the silk kerchief and fold it in half along any one side. Iron out the folding crease. Since silk fabric has a smooth, delicate texture, avoid making large or rough movements during the process. Instead, gently adjust the silk grain (referring to the texture and alignment of the silk threads woven in the warp and weft directions). Note: In the schematic diagrams in Chapter Four, arrows shown as solid lines indicate folding on the front side of the item, while dashed arrows indicate folding on the reverse side.

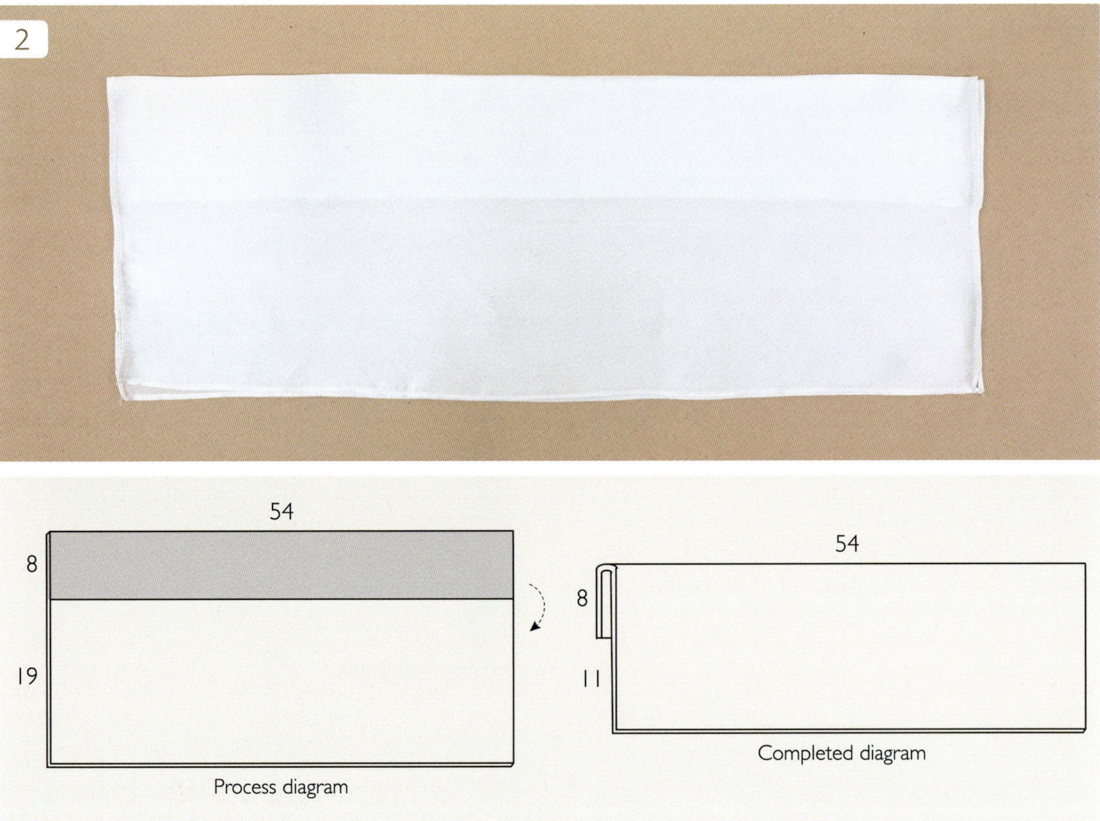

As shown in the schematic diagram, make a backward fold 8 cm down from the top, placing the 8 cm strip behind the 19 cm strip.

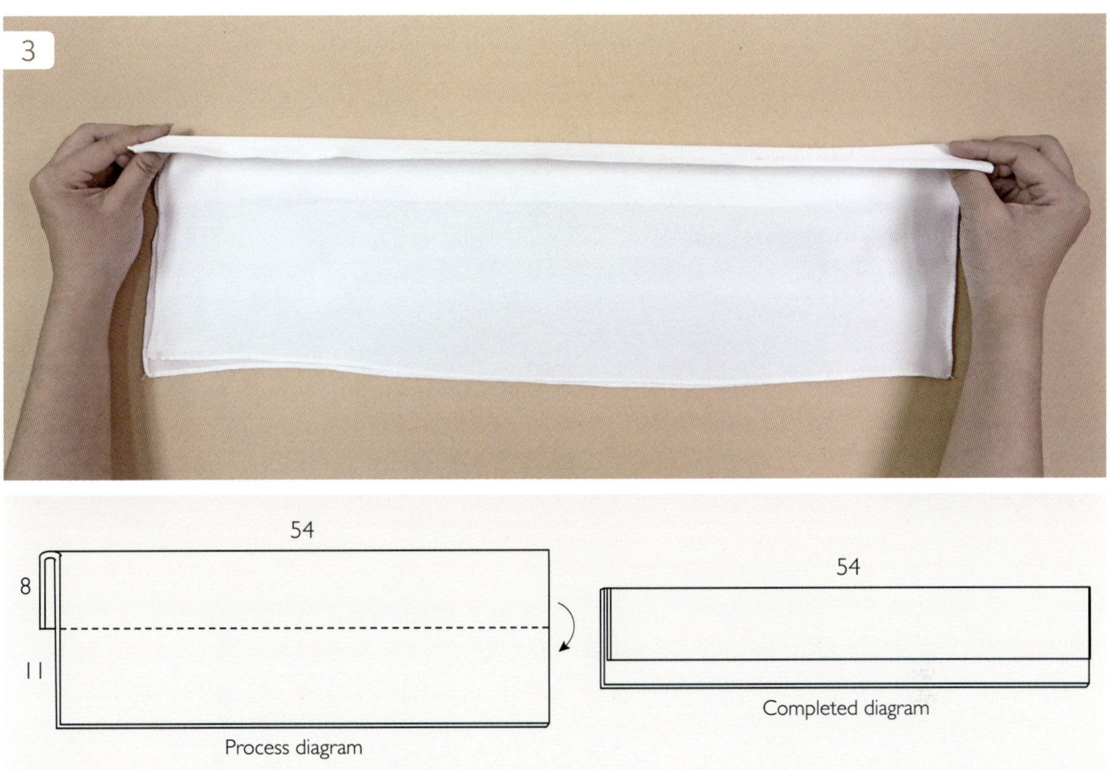

Fold the 8 cm fabric at the top forward along the dashed line. After folding, leave a 3 cm long double layer fabric at the bottom.

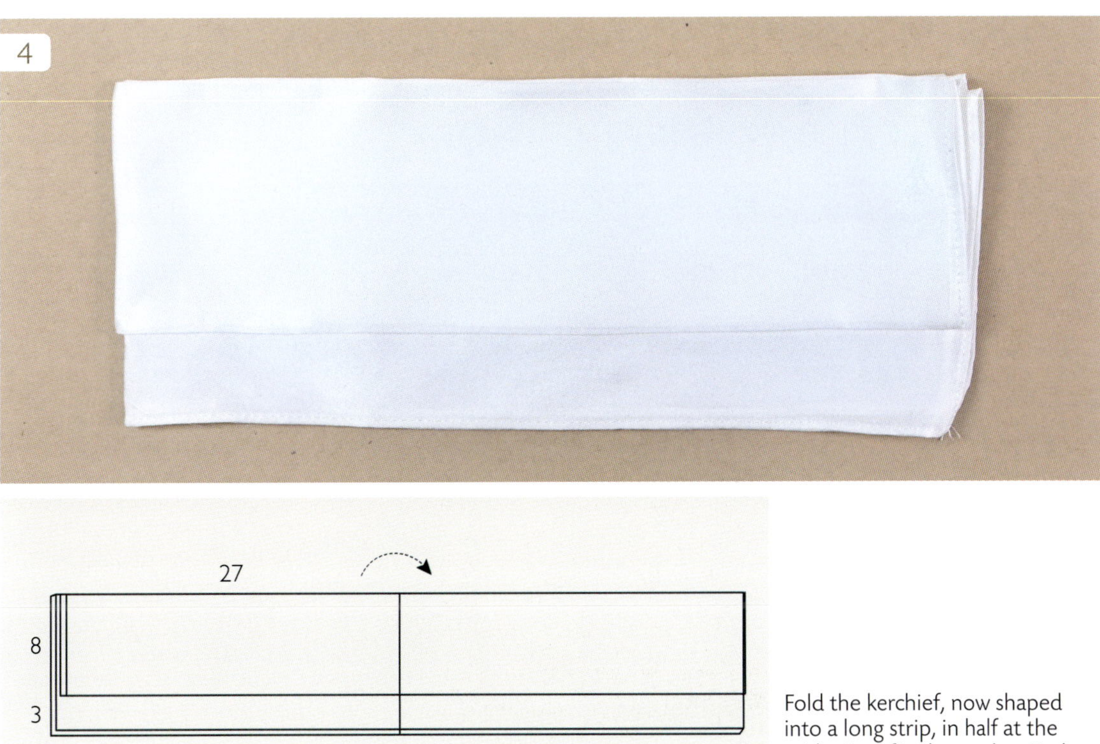

Fold the kerchief, now shaped into a long strip, in half at the midpoint of its long edge. Tuck the left half behind the right half.

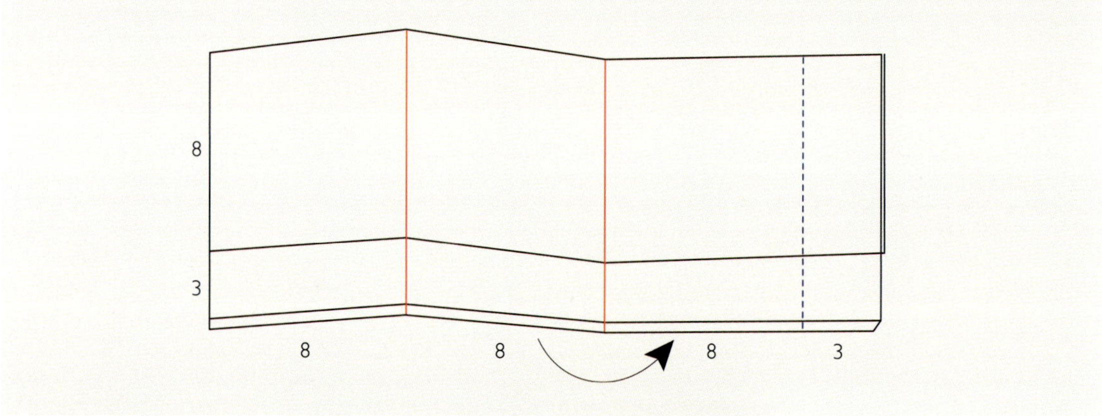

Fold the halved fabric again according to the diagram, with an 8 cm margin. After folding, the solid red line on the far left should align with the dashed blue line, and there should be a 3 cm wide strip of fabric remaining on the right side. Due to the added thickness from folding, the final extra fabric may be slightly less than 3 cm. This is normal. Try to fold evenly and symmetrically to minimize discrepancies. This will ensure that the final dyed pattern appears more regular and visually appealing.

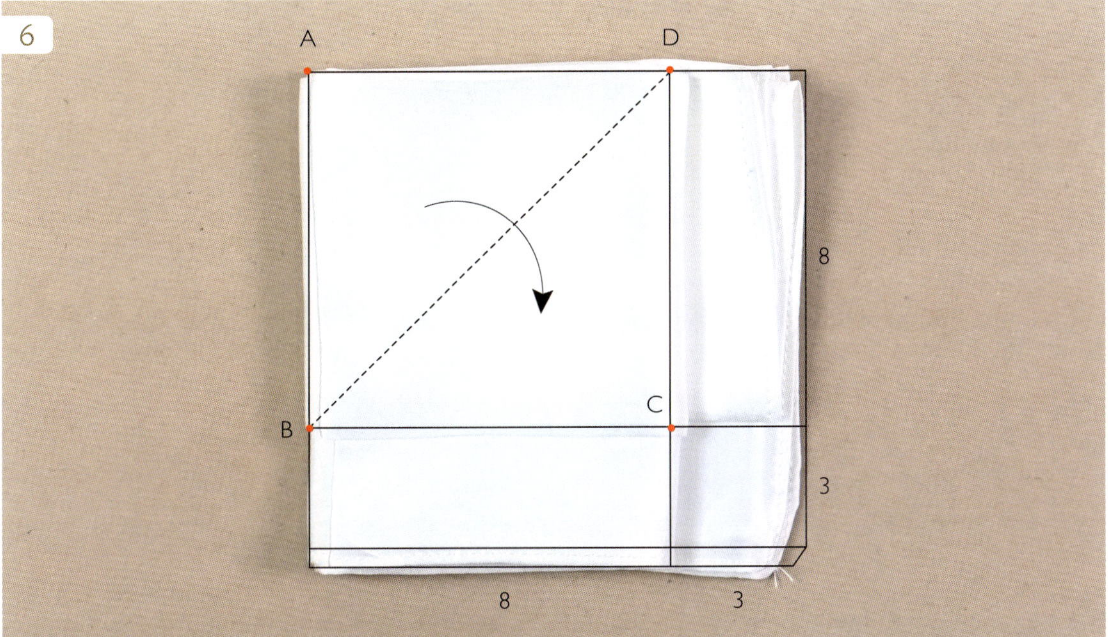

Separate the fabric at point A. Fold both the front and back layers along the BD diagonal toward point C.

Take the wooden boards and, as shown in the diagram, align their two right angled edges with the right angled edges formed by the folded fabric. Use the G-clamp to secure the center of the wooden boards, and fasten the diagonal edges with two binder clips.

Extract 1,000 ml of dye solution using 50 g of amur cork tree, and add 5 g of ferrous sulphate as the mordant. After wetting the tied fabric with clean water, fully immerse it in the dye bath and soak for 4 hours.

Remove the fabric, take off the clips and wooden boards, and rinse to set the dye. Kerchief A is now complete. As shown in the diagram, the wooden boards acted as a resist in the shape of right angled triangles, leaving a regular pattern of white triangles on the fabric. Since the edges of these triangles were not protected by the resist, the dye penetrated those areas directly, creating a grid like effect. A 3 cm-wide yellow green border appears along all four edges of the kerchief. This is the result of the 3 cm fabric margin that was neither folded nor covered by the resist during the earlier steps. In future designs, the creator can adjust the size of this border or eliminate it entirely, depending on the dimensions of the dyed fabric.

❖Kerchief B

Material Preparation

1. One square silk kerchief. This project uses 12 momme pure white silk crepe satin, measuring 54 × 54 cm.
2. Three chopsticks or thin round sticks, each with a diameter of 0.5 cm and a length of at least 15 cm.
3. Three popsicle sticks or wooden slats, each 1 cm wide and at least 12 cm long.
4. Two medium sized binder clips, capable of holding fabric up to 1.5 cm thick.
5. Several rubber bands or tying cords.
6. Dye plant: Safflower.
7. Mordant: Alum.

Steps

Unfold the kerchief. As shown in the diagram, fold the fabric evenly into 8 sections in a fan-like manner. Press the folds with an iron to create folding creases. The final result should be a long rectangular strip of fabric measuring 54 × 6.75 cm.

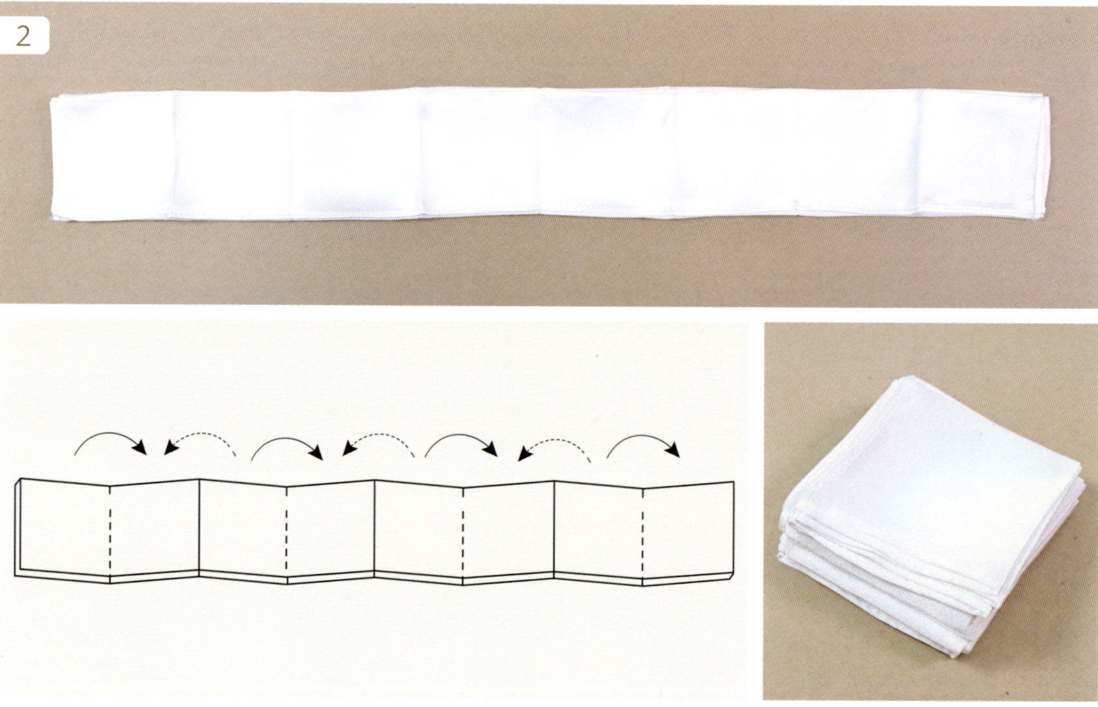

Continue folding the fabric in the same manner as shown in the diagram, dividing it evenly into 8 sections. The final result will be a stack of square fabric pieces, each with a side length of 6.75 cm.

Use a binder clip to attach to one corner of the square fabric piece.

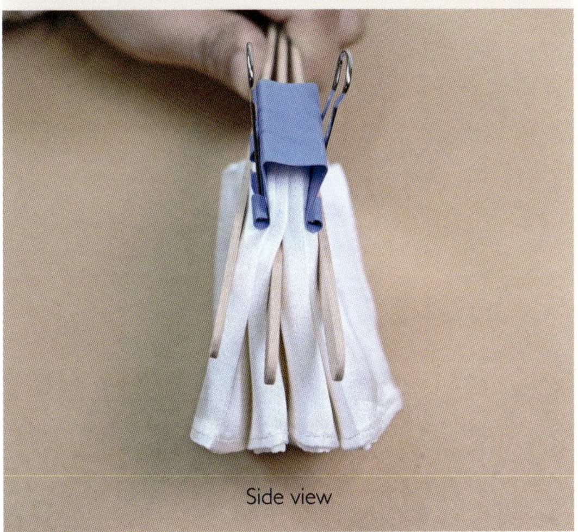

As shown in diagram 4, find the midpoint of two adjacent sides of the square (marked by the red dots). Place three popsicle sticks diagonally as shown in the diagram: two on the outermost edges of the fabric, securing the fabric at the front and back, and one placed at the center of the square stack. This is necessary because the stack has multiple layers, and simply securing the outer edges may result in insufficient resist protection for the middle layers. Use rubber bands or cords to bind both ends of the three popsicle sticks. The silk material is smooth, so try to ensure precise positioning when securing.

Take three wooden chopsticks and place them along the diagonal of the square stack, parallel to the direction of the popsicle sticks. Secure both ends of the chopsticks using the same method as in Step 4. Then, use a binder clip to attach to the corner of the fabric that has not been secured yet.

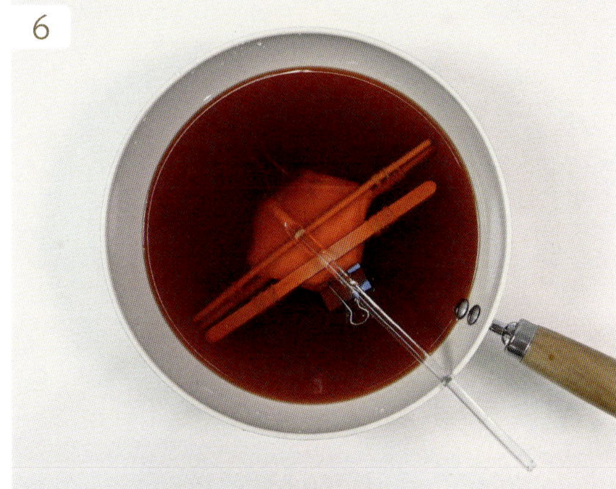

Extract 50 g of safflower to prepare 1,000 ml of dye solution. Add 5 g of alum as the mordant. After wetting the tied fabric with clean water, fully immerse it in the dye solution and soak for 4 hours.

7

Remove the fabric, take off the clips, wooden chopsticks, and popsicle sticks, then wash the fabric. Kerchief B is now complete. When folding the fabric into a square and applying the resist using the wooden sticks, chopsticks, and binder clips, you can adjust the position of the resist or modify the size of the tools. You may also increase or decrease the number of resist tools used. These adjustments will affect the final pattern outcome. Since this project uses silk fabric, which is much lighter and thinner than cotton or linen materials, even though the center of the fabric is treated with resist after folding the edges 8 times, the area is still able to absorb the dye. If using cotton or linen fabric instead, it will enhance the anti-dyeing effect. If you still want to achieve the dyeing effect of silk, you can reduce the number of folds appropriately.

❖Kerchief C

Material Preparation

1. One silk kerchief. This project uses 12 momme pure white silk crepe satin, measuring 54 × 54 cm.
2. Two large wooden clips, two small wooden clips (size can be adjusted based on personal preference).
3. Two medium-sized binder clips, two small binder clips (size can be adjusted based on personal preference).
4. Dye plant: Sappanwood.
5. Mordant: Alum.

Steps

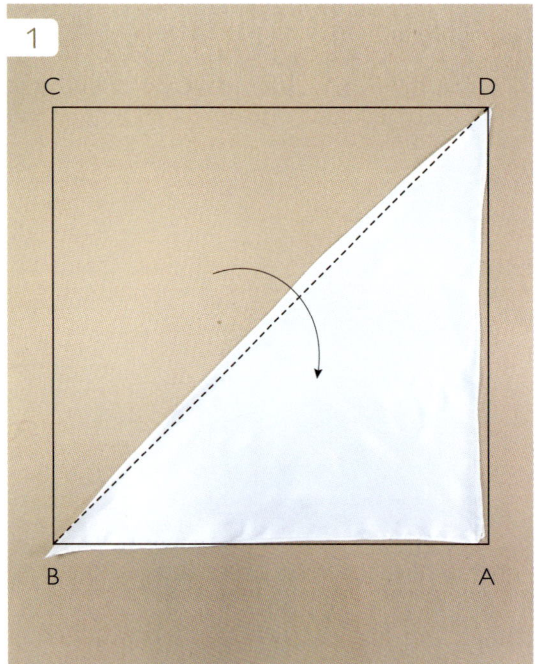

Unfold the silk kerchief. Fold the kerchief diagonally, aligning point C with point A, as shown in the diagram, to form a right angled triangle.

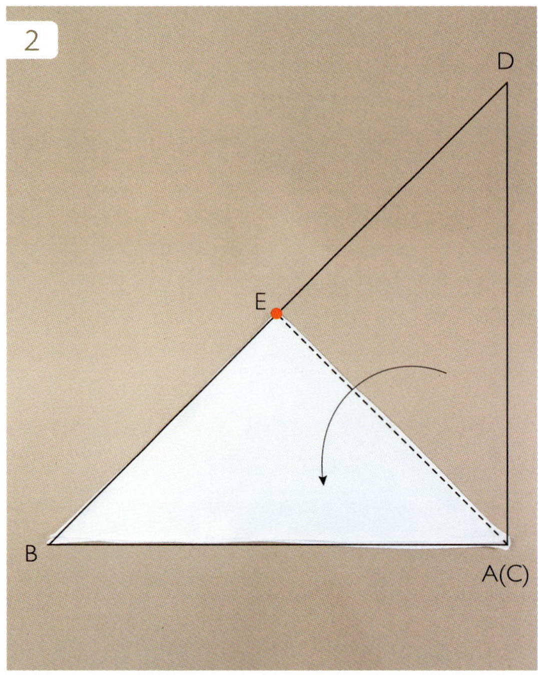

Fold point D along the line segment A (C) E towards point B to form a folding line.

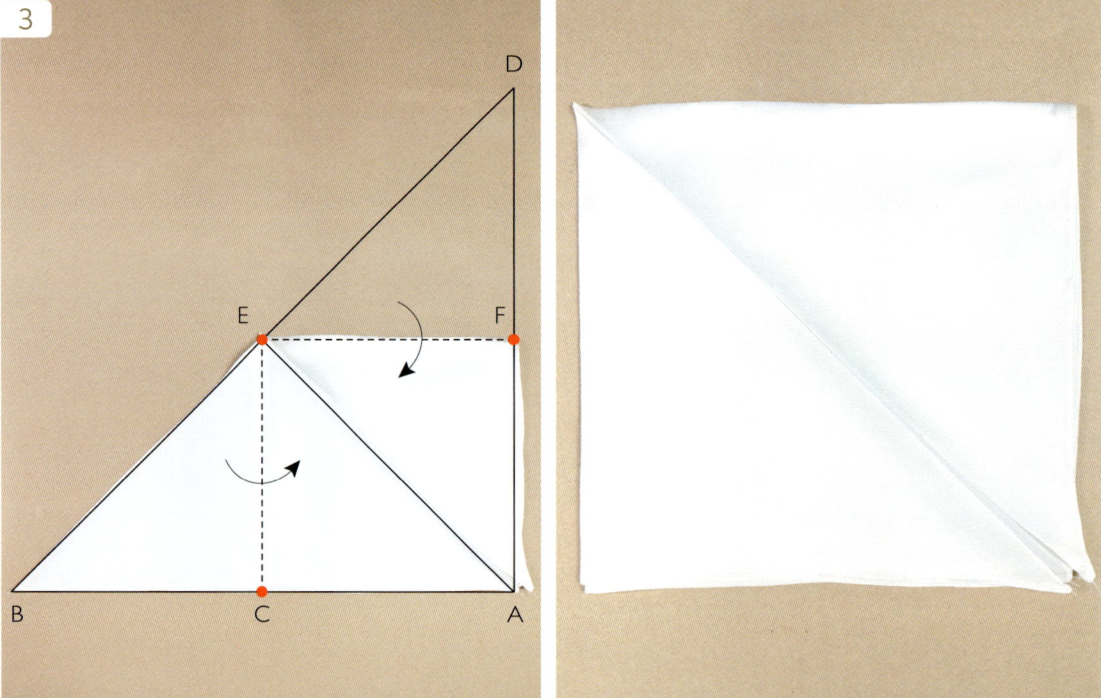

Unfold the fabric from Step 2 and return to the shape from Step 1. Flip the fabric over so that the side with the folding line formed in Step 2 is facing up. As shown in the diagram, fold point B along line segment EC to meet point A, and fold point D along line segment EF to meet point A, forming a square as shown in the right diagram.

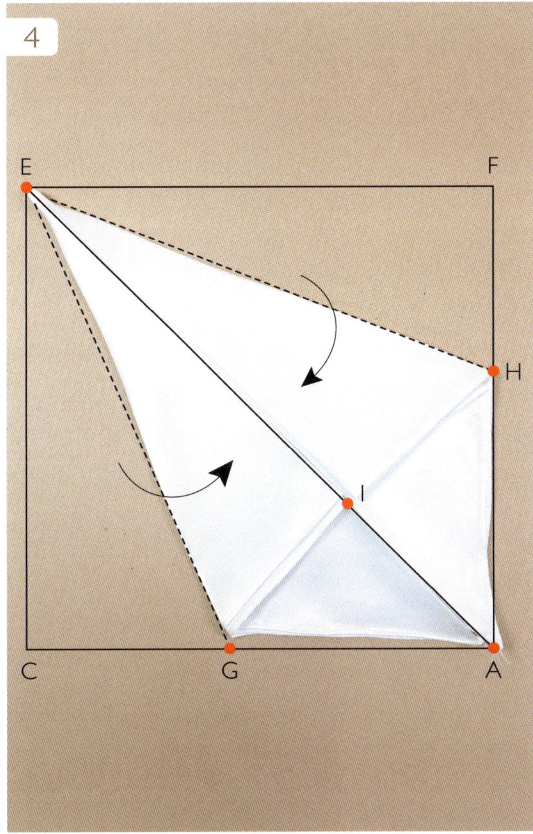

Fold point C along line segment EG to meet point I, and fold point F along line segment EH to meet point I.

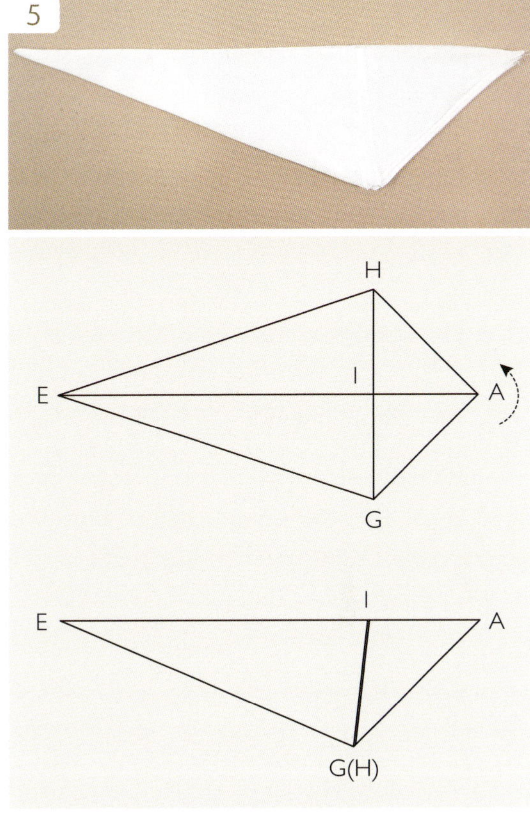

Fold point G from the back along line segment AE to meet point H, flipping the fold outward.

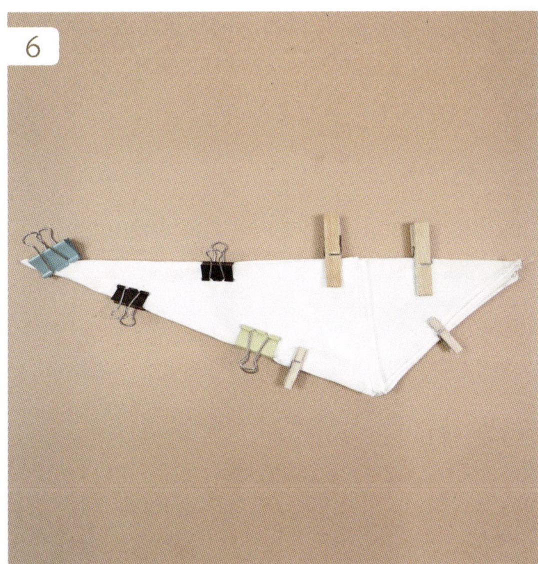

Use binder clips and wooden clips of different sizes for resist dyeing. You can also use other types and sizes of clips. The resist marks formed where the fabric is clipped will vary based on the shape of the clip opening.

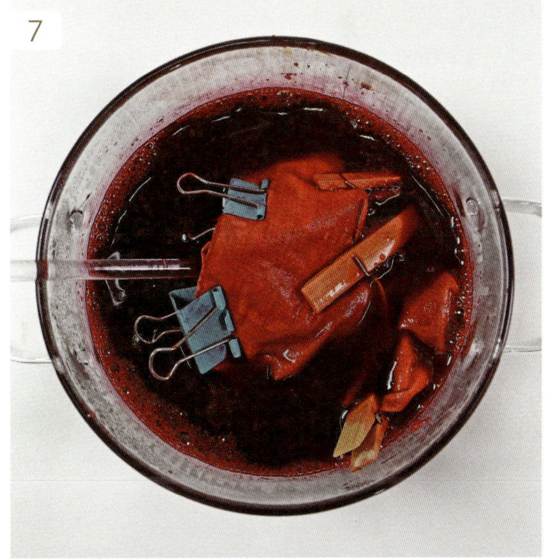

Extract 50 g of sappanwood to prepare 1,000 ml of dye solution. Add 5 g of alum as the mordant. After wetting the tied fabric with clean water, fully immerse it in the dye solution and soak for 4 hours.

8

Remove the fabric, take off the clips, and rinse to fix the color. Kerchief C is now complete. As shown in the diagram, this kerchief features a central radial pattern, divided into 16 equal parts radiating from the center. When creating freely, after completing Steps 1 and 2, you can increase or decrease the number of folds to change the number of divisions. When applying resist with binder clips or wooden clips, you can adjust the resist's position and the size of the tools. You can also increase or decrease the number of tools used. These variations will create a wide range of resist patterns.

Tips

The three projects in the kerchief series are all created through regular folding and the use of auxiliary resist dyeing tools. Regular folding is a crucial technique in tie dyeing. Different folding methods, the same folding method with different resist tools, or the same folding method with varied resist positions can all result in different resist effects. Creators can experiment with more regular, semi-regular, or irregular dyeing techniques based on these foundations.

2. Scarf: *Blue-Green Landscape*

Every time I use cords to bind fabric for tie-dyeing, I am amazed by the beautiful imprints left on the textile, as if the cord has stamped its own unique mark. The texture varies depending on the thickness and material of the cord, creating irregular undulations and flowing patterns through the fabric's folds. This effect resembles the rolling mountain ranges in traditional Chinese landscape paintings, majestic peaks layered upon one another, or the meandering streams, rivers, and lakes nestled among the mountains, evoking a poetic and picturesque scene. This piece is dyed using yellow-green pigment extracted from the amur cork tree, with varied densities of cord binding to create a composition reminiscent of a blue-green landscape painting.

Material Preparation

1. A white scarf, made of silk or pure cotton. This piece uses 5 momme mulberry silk organza fabric, measuring 60 × 200 cm.
2. A cylindrical rod, preferably with a diameter of approximately 2–5 cm and a length of more than 20 cm. This piece uses a solid wooden rod with a diameter of 2.5 cm and a length of 39 cm.
3. Cord, used for tying the fabric. This piece uses 3 mm thick cotton thread.
4. Dye plant: Amur cork tree.
5. Mordant: Ferrous sulphate.
6. Auxiliary tools: Scissors, glass stirring rod, etc.

Steps

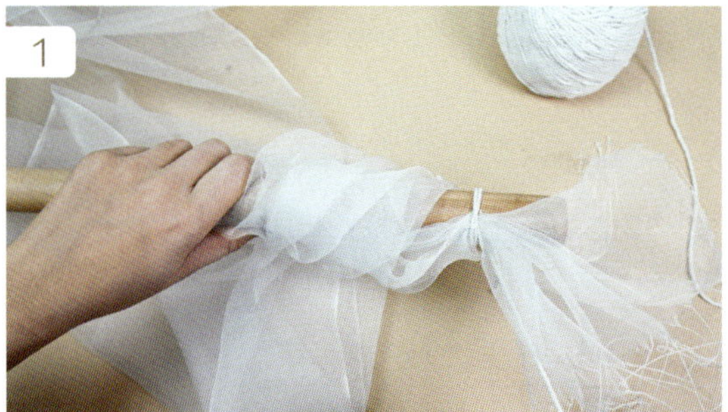

Lay out the scarf with the wide edge as the starting point. At a distance of 10 cm from the edge, evenly fold the short edge of the scarf and wrap it around one end of the wooden rod. Use the cotton cord to tie 2–3 loops to secure the edge of the scarf, then tighten and knot it.

Wrap the scarf around the outer circumference of the wooden rod. Since the width of the scarf is longer than the circumference of the rod, you may need to fold the scarf slightly during the wrapping. It is recommended to fold it irregularly and freely. When wrapping with the cotton cord, adjust the spacing between the lines to create a varying density, resulting in an effect of wide and narrow bindings. This will help form a high and low, continuous, undulating mountain range in the final piece. Be sure to pull each loop of the cord tightly to ensure the dye resistance effect.

Continue wrapping the scarf for about 20 cm as described in Step 2. Then, pull the cord tight and tie a knot to finish the binding on one side.

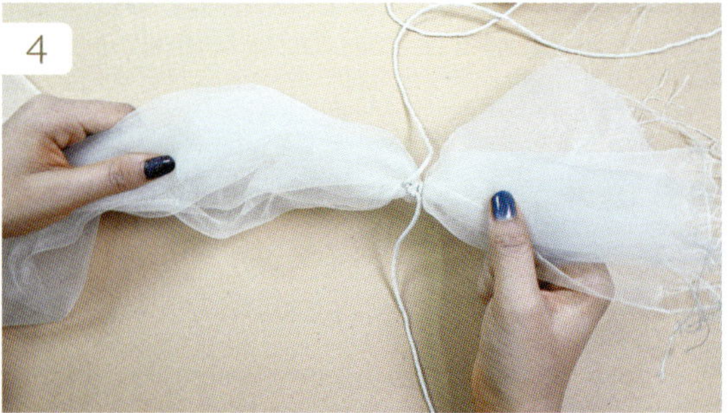

For the other side of the scarf, there is no need for the wooden rod. Instead, about 15 cm from the edge, tie a knot with the cotton cord. Hold the scarf at the knot with one hand and use the other hand to rotate and tighten the scarf.

Use the cotton cord to tightly bind the scarf in a circular fashion. When wrapping, avoid making the coils too tight to avoid excessive resist dyeing, which could result in missing patterns. Similarly, pay attention to the variation in spacing between each coil of the cord. The more evenly the cotton cord is wrapped, the more uniform the final tie-dye pattern will be.

Continue wrapping the scarf for about 40 cm using the method from Step 5, then pull the cord tight and tie a knot to finish the binding on this side.

The result of the scarf binding is shown in the image.

Prepare 1,000 ml of extract dye with 250 g of the amur cork tree, adding 3 g of ferrous sulphate and stirring until dissolved. Place the mixture in a container, preferably a tall cylindrical one, so that the scarf bound on the wooden rod can be fully submerged in the dye. Completely soak the scarf in clean water, then wring it out gently. Slowly place it into the dye solution and let it sit for 24 hours. During this time, stir the fabric several times to ensure it absorbs the dye thoroughly.

Tips

This piece demonstrates how to use the tying technique with cord to create tie-dye artwork. This method offers a high degree of flexibility and can be adapted in various ways during the later stages of the creative process. Using cords of different materials and textures can create distinct marks on the fabric. Even the same type of cord can leave different imprints depending on the fabric's material and density. This provides a foundation for more in-depth and detailed experimentation.

Remove the scarf from the dye bath, undo the cotton cord, and wash away any excess dye. Then, perform a color-setting treatment (see page 37), completing the dyeing of the piece. For this scarf, two different tying methods were used at both ends. One end was wrapped around the wooden rod, creating clear, undulating lines, while the other end relied solely on the cord to create a fusion effect between the lines and the block areas. The lines are denser, and the transitions and layers are richer. The final result will vary with slight changes in technique.

3. Tote Bag: *Night City*

This tote bag features a pattern that captures the scene of a city at night. The black and gray tones of the image evoke a serene, tranquil night, steady and mysterious, as if isolating the hustle and bustle of the city from the view. The white squares and long strips scattered across the design resemble the lights of countless homes, twinkling like stars, warm and bright, adding a touch of human warmth to the tranquility. The folded line patterns on the bag's body mimic the ripples on the water's surface, light and undulating, with clear layers, as if telling the story of nature's forces and the passage of time.

Material Preparation

1. White cotton fabric: 2 pieces, each 45 × 100 cm (for the handbag's outer and lining fabric); 2 pieces, each 15 × 70 cm (for the bag handles).
2. A variety of wood clips and binder clips, no specific size requirement.
3. Several wooden sticks or ice cream sticks: 1 cm and 2 cm wide, with a length greater than 10 cm.
4. Several rubber bands, paper clips, and wooden chopsticks.
5. Dyeing plant: Tea leaves (no restrictions on variety or origin), this work on display specifically using Zhengshan Xiaozhong black tea from Fujian, China.
6. Mordant: Yellow alum.
7. Auxiliary tools: Scissors, ruler, water soluble fabric pen, sewing needle, sewing thread, strong clips, iron, etc.

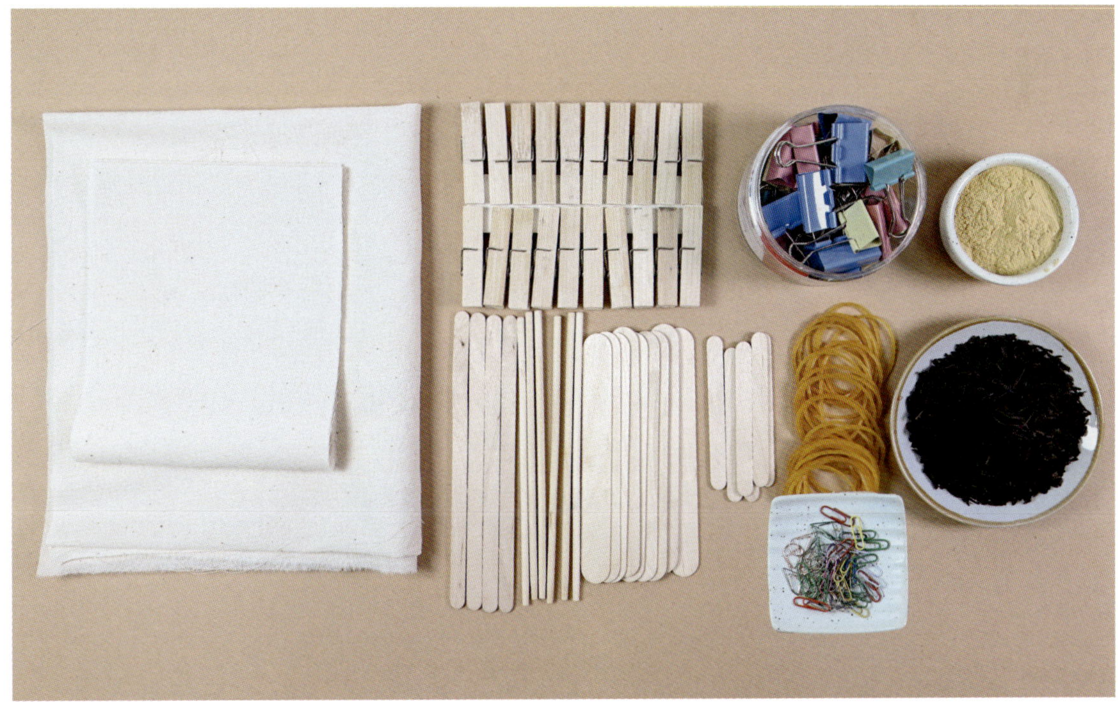

Steps

1

Take one piece of 45 × 100 cm cotton fabric and evenly fold it into 6 sections in a fan shape. Take two pieces of 15 × 70 cm cotton fabric and fold each piece in half once.

As shown in diagram 2, use tools such as ice cream sticks, chopsticks, paper clips, and wood clips to secure the fabric. Arrange them according to the positions, spacing, and angles shown in the diagram at the bottom. Note that the shorter fabric pieces are for the handles. When performing the resist dyeing process, make sure the two folded fabric pieces are completely overlapping. When using ice cream sticks and chopsticks, you need to use two at the same time, placing them on the top and bottom of the fabric in the same position to achieve the resist effect. Secure both sides with rubber bands or binder clips. When using paper clips, since their clamping force is weaker, manually press the paper clips to make them tighter.

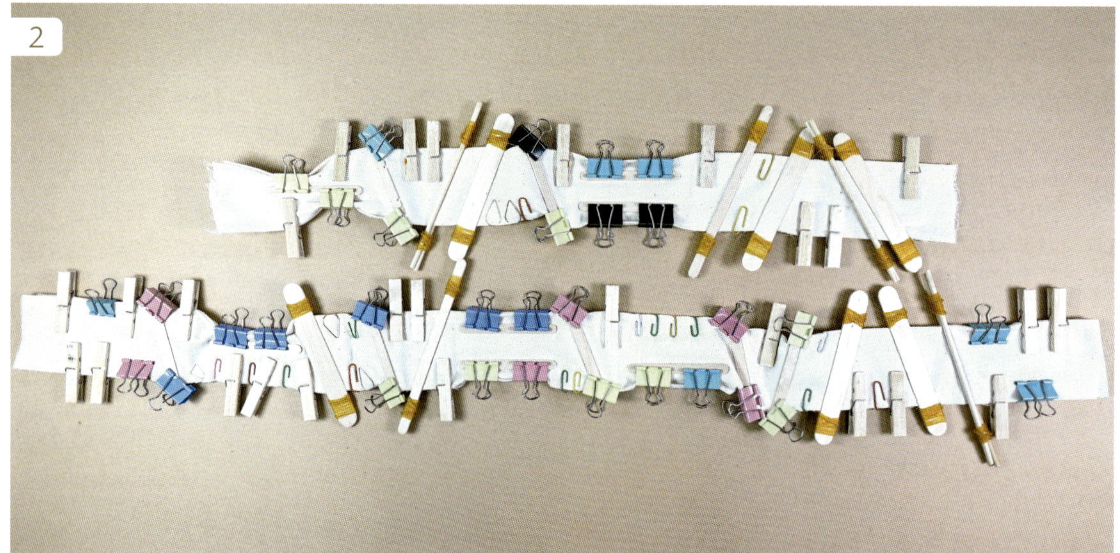
2

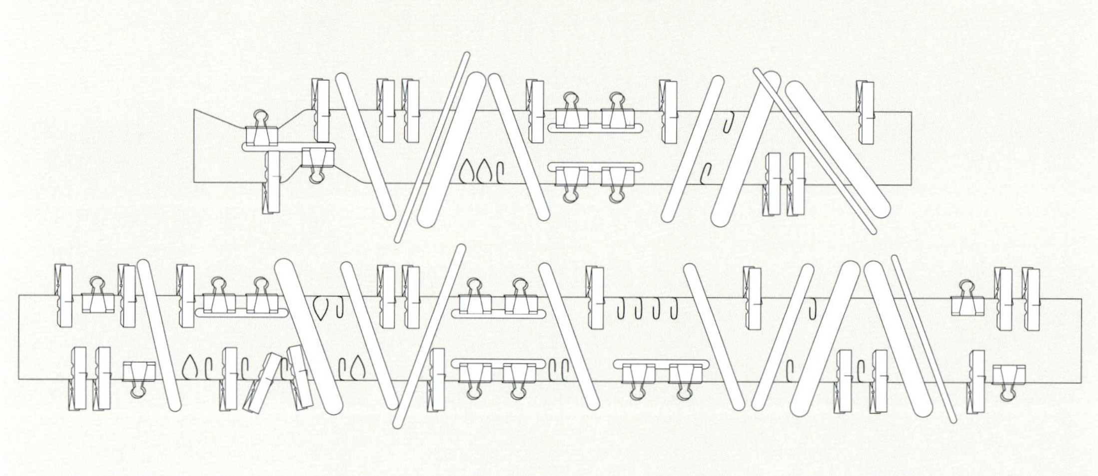

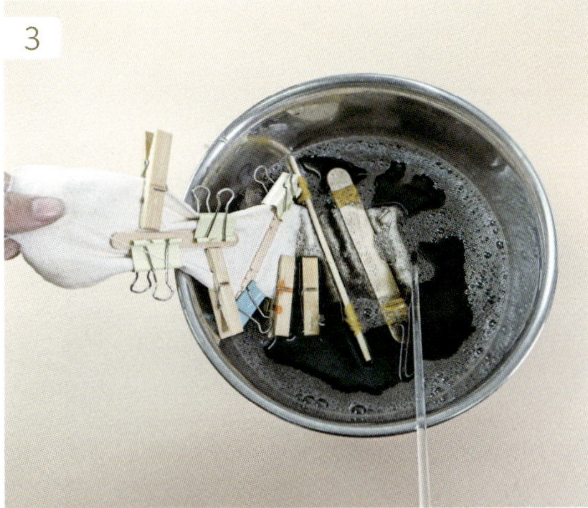

Prepare a dye solution by extracting 250 g of black tea into 4 L of water, and add 10 to 15 g of yellow alum mordant, stirring until well mixed. After wetting the fabric treated with resist dyeing in Step 2, as well as the lining fabric, place them into the dye solution and let them soak for 4 hours. After soaking, gently rinse the fabric to remove any excess dye, but do not remove the clips or other tools. Allow the fabric to dry, then soak it again for 4 hours. Repeat this process 4 or 5 times. The more times you repeat it, the deeper the color and the clearer the resist-dyed pattern will be.

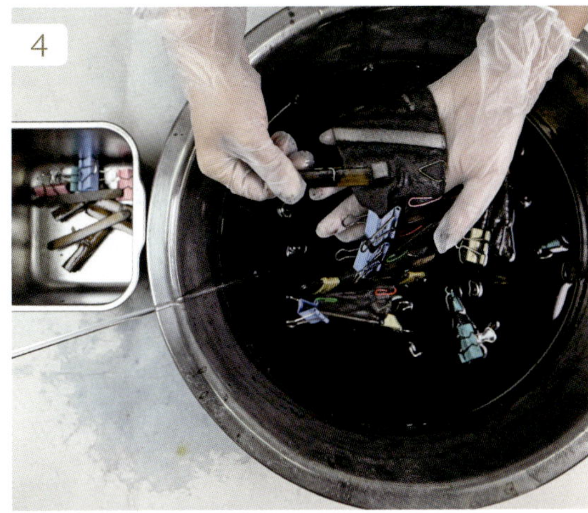

After the dyeing is complete, remove the wood clips, paper clips, and other tools, then wash the fabric and perform a color fixation treatment.

Cut the outer fabric and lining fabric to a size of 42 × 92 cm, and the two handle pieces to a size of 10 × 60 cm. As shown in the diagram, the lining fabric is not subjected to the fold dyeing process, resulting in a darker color compared to the outer fabric and handle fabric. During production, you can also control the different dyeing times for the outer fabric and lining fabric to achieve a color contrast between the two, or you can choose pre-colored cotton fabric, which eliminates the need to dye the lining fabric.

6

Determine the front and back of the outer fabric based on personal preference. Fold the outer fabric along the long edge, with the back side facing out and the front side facing in. As shown in the diagram, sew both sides, keeping a 1 cm seam allowance, and start sewing 0.5 cm from the top edge, ensuring that the bottom seam is as close to the end as possible. For the lining fabric, the process is the same as for the outer fabric. When sewing the lining, sew one side completely, leaving a 10 to 15 cm gap (called the "turning hole") unsewn in the middle on the other side. A turning hole is an unsewn section left on purpose so that the sewn fabric can be smoothly turned right side out. Once turned, the turning hole should be sewn closed using either a sewing machine or hand stitching. You can sew by hand or with a machine. Be sure to backstitch at the start and end to prevent the knots from being pulled through the fabric when tightening the thread. When hand stitching, aim for 8 to 9 stitches per 3 cm.

Take the handle fabric and fold it along the short edge, with the front side facing inward and the back side facing outward. Sew along the long edge with a 1 cm seam allowance to form a long strip, as shown in the diagram. Repeat the same process for the other handle fabric.

Turn the handle fabric right side out. To do this, turn it in small sections at a time, and you may use tools like tweezers to assist with the turning process. Once turned, make sure the seam is pushed to the edge to ensure the handle width is consistent. Press the fabric flat with an iron to smooth it out.

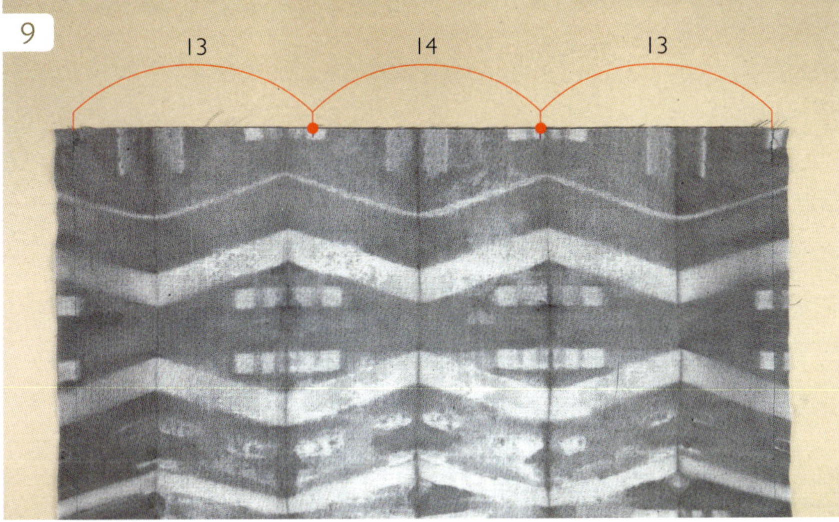

Take the outer fabric with the back side facing out. As shown in the diagram, use a water-soluble pen to mark two reference points along the top edge of the fabric.

Turn the outer fabric right side out. Place the handles on the outer fabric at the marked reference points, aligning the edges of the handles with the top edge of the outer fabric. Use clips or pins to hold the fabric in place. Sew the fabric and handles together, keeping the seam approximately 0.5 cm from the edge. Attach one handle to the front side and the other to the back side of the outer fabric.

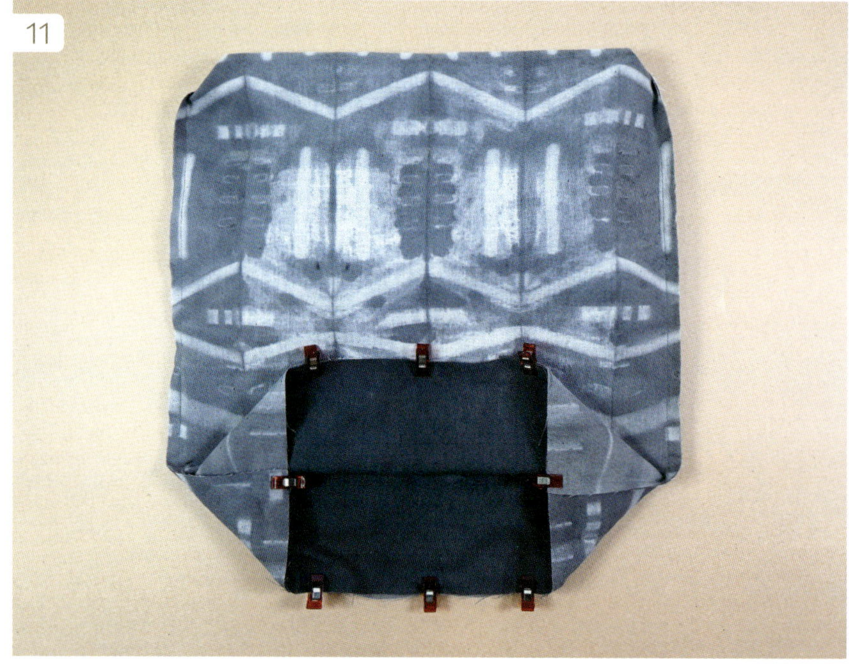

Turn the outer fabric to have the back side facing out and the lining fabric with the front side facing out. Slip the outer fabric over the lining fabric, ensuring that the handles naturally hang in the middle of the outer and lining fabrics. Align the top edges of both fabrics and secure them with clips or pins. Sew along the top edge of the fabrics, maintaining a seam allowance of 1 cm.

At this point, the outer and lining fabrics are completely sewn together with the back side facing out. Pull the outer fabric and lining fabric through the turning hole (marked with the red curved line) in the lining fabric, turning them right side out.

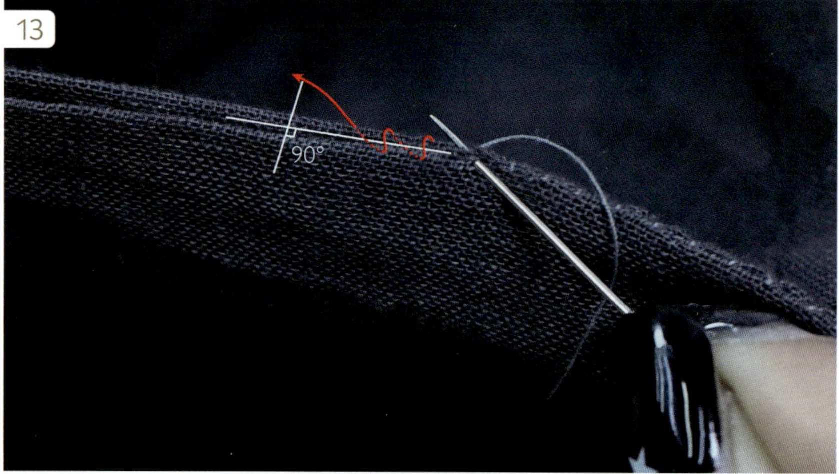

Use a hidden stitch to sew the turning hole closed. Use a sewing thread that closely matches the color of the lining fabric. Start by inserting the needle from the lower fabric, then angle it out through the upper fabric. Each time you insert and remove the needle, pick up 2 to 3 threads of fabric. This technique helps to better hide the stitching line.

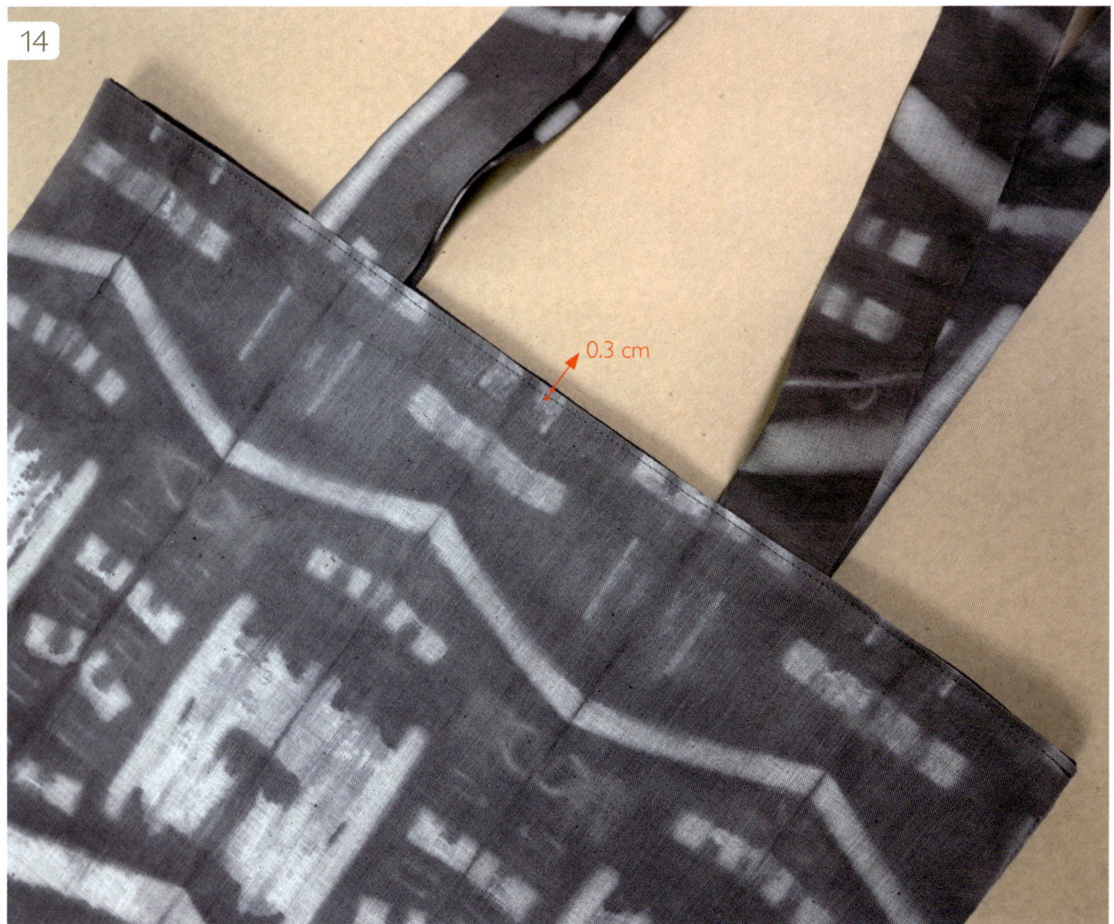

Insert the lining into the outer fabric, and adjust the top edge seam allowance as well as the folded corners at the base of the bag. Sew a line of stitching about 0.3 cm from the top edge. This will help the top edge to remain neat and crisp. The tote bag is now complete.

Tips

The resist dyeing technique used in this project provides the creator with a method to handle long fabrics through tie dye folding. During the creative process, the positions, distances, and angles of clips, boards, and paperclips can be freely arranged. Different combinations of these elements can create countless pattern variations. This technique can also be applied not only to the design of tote bags but also to the creation of other home goods and daily items.

There are a few points that readers should pay attention to:

First, the fabric in the middle of the fold will be more difficult to dye when using the folding method for resist-dyeing. Therefore, it is not advisable to fold the fabric too many times. A fan folding method is the best choice. If the fabric is folded too many times or wrapped, the fabric closer to the center will be harder to dye.

Second, plant based dyes have lower molecular activity, making them more difficult to dye on cotton and linen materials compared to silk and wool. Additionally, after folding, the dyeing difficulty increases, and the color will be much lighter than on a single layer of fabric. If creators wish to replace plant based dyes, it is recommended to use darker colored dyes or indigo dye, or to choose relatively thinner fabrics with a looser weave.

4. Placemat: *Turtle's Blessing*

This project is inspired by the traditional turtle shell pattern in Chinese culture. The turtle is considered a symbol of longevity and good fortune, and the turtle shell pattern embodies wishes for health, long life, and well being. The pattern in this project simulates the geometric texture of a turtle's shell, using hexagons as the basic unit and incorporating circles and triangles that expand outward in a continuous manner. In terms of production technique, this project utilizes stencil resist dyeing technology, where the precise carving of the stencil and accurate resist dyeing process clearly outline the design's contours.

Material Preparation

1. Kraft paper: 1 sheet, size 30 × 30 cm.
2. White cotton fabric: 2 pieces, each 30 × 30 cm, for the front and back fabric.
3. Single side adhesive cotton batting interlining: 1 piece, size 25 × 25 cm.
4. 30 ml tung oil and a tung oil brush.
5. Scraper: Small size.
6. Soybean flour: 20 g.
7. Lime powder: 20 g.
8. Indigo dye: 30 g, along with alkaline agents and reducing agents.
9. Auxiliary tools: Carving knife, scissors, sewing thread, sewing needles, ruler, pencil, iron, etc.

Steps

Make the stencil. With a compass and ruler, draw the pattern on the kraft paper, centering it according to the reference image. Start by drawing all the reference lines based on the intervals and angles indicated in the reference line diagram (see page 165). Then, following the complete reference diagram (see page 166), connect the reference lines to form the complete design.

Carve the pattern on the stencil by cutting along the lines. When using the carving knife, gently score along the lines first to create indentations, then apply more pressure to cut through. This technique helps make the lines smoother. The book provides pattern templates, which can be transferred and carved using a cutting machine, eliminating the need to complete Steps 1 and 2.

Apply tung oil. Dip the brush into the tung oil and brush the stencil from top to bottom and from left to right. Once the entire surface of the kraft paper is covered with tung oil, wait for about 1 minute to allow the paper to fully absorb the oil. Then, flip the paper over and apply tung oil in the same manner on the other side. The kraft paper will change from light coffee color to dark coffee color. If there are areas on the kraft paper that still appear light coffee color and granular, it indicates that those areas haven't fully absorbed the tung oil and should be brushed again in those specific areas.

Dry the stencil. Clip the stencil and hang it in a shaded area indoors to air dry. After the first coat of tung oil is applied, the tung oil on the kraft paper will be relatively thin and will not fully waterproof the paper. Therefore, repeat the process from Step 3 by applying a second coat of tung oil and letting it dry in the shade again. This will complete the creation of the stencil.

Mix 20 g each of soybean flour and lime powder. Add 52 ml of clean water and stir to form a paste. The ratio of soybean flour to lime powder should be 1:1, and the total weight of the two powders and water should be mixed in a 10:13 ratio. Adjust the amount of water based on the thickness of the fabric. If the fabric is thick, you can add more water. Otherwise, if the soybean paste is too thick, it will reduce its adhesion to the fabric. For thinner fabrics, you can reduce the amount of water appropriately.

Once the soybean-lime mixture has been stirred to the consistency shown in the diagram, you can proceed to the next step.

Apply the paste. Iron the fabric smooth and place it on the table. Center the stencil on the fabric. Dip the scraper into the paste and apply it in a downward and left to right direction. During the process, press the stencil with one hand to prevent it from moving. You can also use tape to secure the stencil before applying the paste. With the other hand, maintain a 45-degree angle between the scraper and the surface of the stencil. It is recommended to apply three coats of paste to achieve a thickness of approximately 1 to 2 mm. This will ensure that the paste adheres firmly to the fabric, enhancing the resist dyeing effect. Otherwise, dye may still seep through tiny gaps in the paste.

Remove the stencil. After applying the paste, press down on the fabric with one hand while gently lifting the stencil with the other hand. This action should be done slowly and carefully to avoid accidentally spreading the paste to areas that haven't been treated with the resist. Once the stencil is removed, it should be cleaned and dried promptly for long term storage and reuse.

Hang the fabric indoors to air dry. If the fabric is thick, after applying the paste, you can use a spray bottle to lightly spray the inside of the fabric with an appropriate amount of water to ensure the paste fully penetrates.

Once the fabric has air-dried, it is ready for the dyeing process. The dried fabric may appear wrinkled and this is normal. Do not pull or stretch the fabric, as it may cause the paste to crack and compromise the resist dyeing effect. Soak the dried fabric in clean water for 10 to 20 minutes. Once it is fully saturated, you can proceed with dyeing.

Prepare the indigo dye solution. Submerge the fabric vertically into the dye bath. The number of dyeing repetitions can be adjusted according to the desired depth of blue. The back fabric can be dyed at the same time.

Remove the fabric, rinse off excess dye with clean water, and hang it to dry.

Remove the resist paste. Once both the fabric and the paste are completely dry, gently pull the fabric in three directions: horizontal, vertical, and at a 45-degree diagonal. This will cause the dried paste to crack. Use a scraper to gently lift off the paste. Avoid applying excessive force to prevent damaging the fabric.

Trim the front and back fabrics to 27 × 27 cm, and the single side cotton batting interlining to 25 × 25 cm. You can now begin the placemat assembly stage.

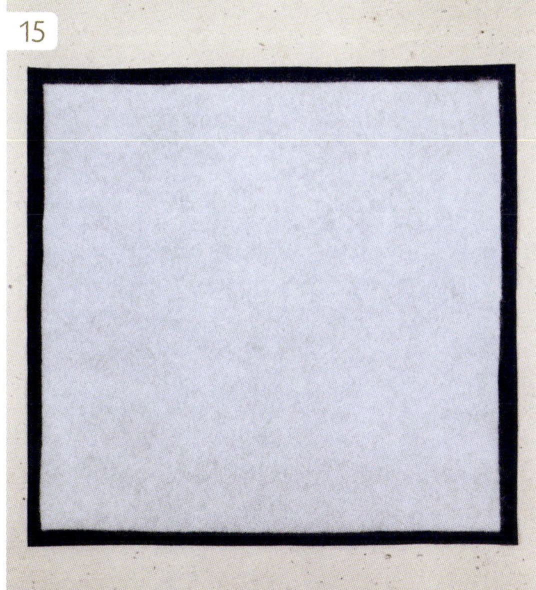

Adhere the front fabric to the single side cotton batting interlining. Center the single side cotton batting interlining on the front fabric. One side of the batting has adhesive dots, while the other side is smooth. Place the adhesive side against the back of the front fabric and secure it in place with pins. Using an iron, press from the front side of the fabric to heat fuse the two layers. Be careful not to press too hard with the iron, as this can flatten the padding and reduce its fluffiness.

Align the front fabric and back fabric with right sides facing each other. Sew along all four edges, maintaining a 1 cm seam allowance. Be sure to leave a 10 cm turning hole on one side unstitched. This will be used to turn the piece right side out later.

Turn the fabric right side out through the turning hole. While turning, carefully manage the corners to ensure they lie flat and neat once flipped. Begin with any one corner. Fold one seam allowance edge inward toward the side with the interfacing cotton batting, following the stitched seam. Then fold the adjacent seam allowance edge in the same way to form a 90-degree angle. This ensures the fabric edges wrap neatly around the corner. Pinch the prepared corner and gently pull it through the turning hole. This method helps prevent excessive bulk from gathering at the tip of the corners.

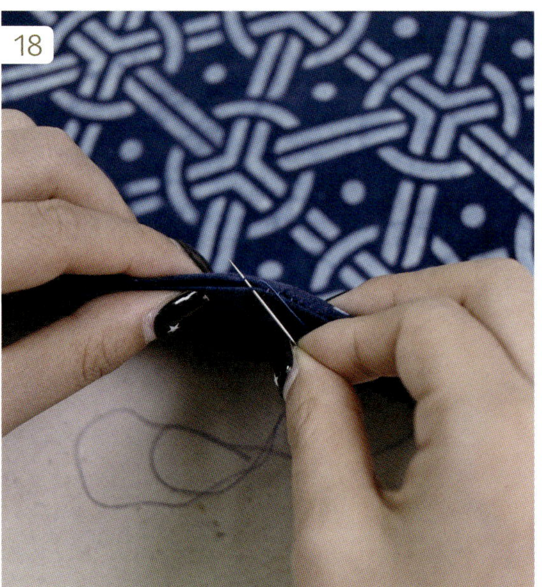

Use the hidden stitch to sew up the turning hole. Select a thread color that closely matches the front fabric. Refer to Step 13 on page 120 for instructions on the hidden stitch technique.

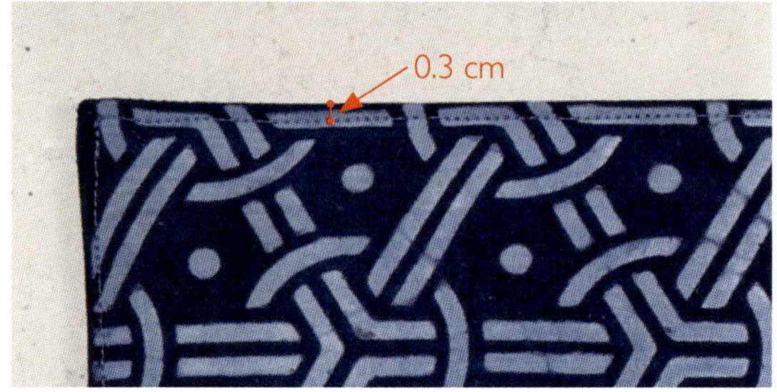

Iron the placemat. Then, sew a line around the edge of the placemat, approximately 0.3 cm from the border, to flatten and neaten the edges of the front and back fabrics. The placemat is now complete.

Tips

Creators are free to design your own stencils for dyeing. However, the hollow areas of the stencil should not be too large or overly elongated in shape, or the stencil may curl during paste application and lead to uneven spreading of the paste.

Soybean flour and lime powder should be stored separately and kept away from light. If the prepared resist paste made by mixing with water is not used up on the same day, it can be covered with plastic wrap and used the following day. If the paste becomes dry during use, a small amount of water can be added to re-mix it.

Soybean paste is suitable for cotton and linen fabrics, while glutinous rice paste is better for silk fabrics. Stencil dyeing is not suitable for all plant-based dyes. It works best with indigo dye, which can only be applied cold and must not be heated during the dyeing process.

5. Book Cover: *Possessing Abundant Knowledge*

This project is inspired by traditional Chinese fish motifs. In Chinese, the word for "fish (鱼, *yú*)" is a homophone for "abundance (余, *yú*)." The implied meaning of the image of a fish is thus "abundance year after year" and "abundance of prosperity," symbolizing abundance and happiness. It is a traditional symbol of good fortune that has been passed down in China for millennia. Since ancient times, the fish motif has frequently appeared on jade and bronze artifacts, embodying the ancestors' hopes for a good and prosperous life.

In this creation, the artist reinterprets those classic fish motifs through the wax dyeing technique. The chosen color palette features a warm yellow tone derived from gardenia dye. In traditional Chinese culture, yellow symbolizes harvest, hope, and wealth, resonating with the auspicious meaning of the fish motif. At the same time, the vibrant hue conveys a sense of brightness and positivity, infusing the book cover with a blend of traditional charm and contemporary style.

Material Preparation

1. Two pieces of white cotton fabric, each measuring 75 × 40 cm.
2. Pattern sheet, 40 × 26 cm(the pattern template can be found on page 167. This cover is designed for B5 size notebooks—other sizes can be adapted by proportionally scaling or rearranging the design).
3. Small wax knife, electric stove, wax melting pot and paraffin wax.
4. Medium weight fusible interfacing, 75 × 40 cm.
5. Dye plant: Gardenia.
6. Auxiliary tools: Heat erasable pen, light box, scissors, ruler, sewing needles, sewing thread, iron, etc.

Tips for Applying Wax

Before applying wax, place a plastic sheet under the fabric to prevent wax from seeping through to the table surface. Beginners can use a fan shaped wax knife, and it is helpful to prepare a wax absorbing cloth. You can use leftover fabric scraps from cutting.

When applying wax, dip the wax knife into the melted wax for 3 to 5 seconds to preheat it. After lightly dipping it in wax, first wipe it on the wax absorbing cloth so that some of the wax is absorbed before you begin drawing. This prevents excess wax from spreading too much on the fabric surface. When applying wax, use the tip of the wax knife to draw fine details, and the side of the knife to outline curved contours.

After waxing, flip the fabric over to check the back. If some areas are properly resist-dyed on the front but not on the back, you can apply wax again on the back to ensure complete coverage. Maintain the wax temperature between 60 to 85°C. If the temperature is too high, it will produce excessive smoke and a pungent odor. If too low, the wax will lack penetration, making it prone to flaking off and resulting in poor resist dyeing performance.

Steps

Align the white fabric and the pattern sheet at the center, with the fabric on top and the pattern underneath. Place them on a light box and trace along the black contour lines. If a light box is not available, you can tape the fabric and pattern to a glass window and use sunlight to trace. Use a heat erasable pen during the tracing process.

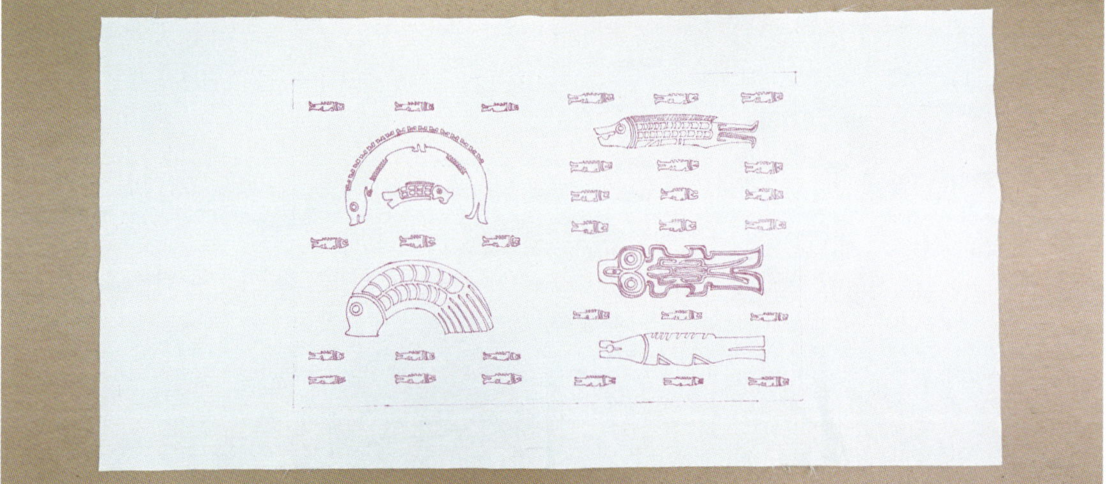

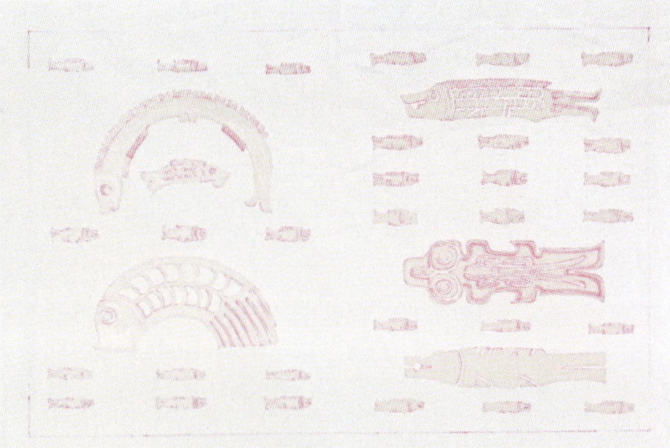

2

Melt the wax. This project uses pure paraffin wax, which has a clean white appearance and produces better results when dyeing yellow with gardenia. Apply wax to all the black filled areas on the pattern sheet using the molten wax.

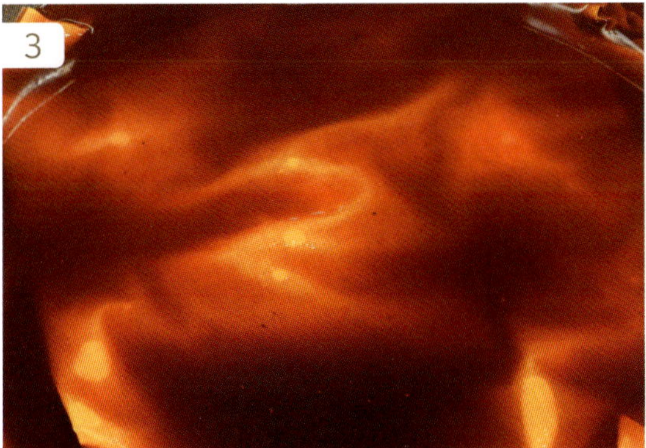

3

Extract approximately 3 L of dye solution from 150 g of gardenia, then add 3 L of clean water to make a total of 6 L of dye solution. Wet both the wax resist fabric and another piece of plain white fabric, then place them into the dye solution to soak for 2 hours. When wetting the wax resist fabric, make sure it lies flat and do not rub it, as doing so may cause the sealed paraffin to crack, resulting in fractures through which dye can seep into the resist areas. During the first 10 minutes of soaking, continuously stir the fabric to ensure even dyeing.

4

Remove the fabric from the dye bath, rinse with water to wash off excess dye. You may gently rub the fabric during washing. Hang to dry indoors.

5

Prepare newspaper, *xuan* paper, or other wax-absorbent paper. Once the fabric is completely dry, proceed to remove the wax. Place 2 to 3 layers of paper both above and below the fabric, and iron it. Under high heat, the wax melts and is absorbed into the paper. This method may leave a small amount of wax residue in the gaps between the interwoven threads of the fabric. After wax removal, the fabric may become stiff, and the areas surrounding the waxed patterns may appear darker due to residual wax.

Making the book cover. Iron the two pieces of yellow dyed fabric flat and cut them to a size of 62 × 29 cm, ensuring that the wax dye pattern is centered. The fabric with the wax dye pattern will be the outer cover of the book, while the plain fabric will be the inner lining. Also, cut the interfacing fabric to the same dimensions as the outer and inner covers of the book.

Attach the outer fabric to the interfacing. The interfacing helps increase the fabric's stiffness. One side is smooth, while the other has shiny adhesive particles. After applying high-temperature ironing, the adhesive particles melt and bond the interfacing to the fabric. Place the adhesive side of the interfacing onto the back of the wax dyed fabric and iron, starting from the center and working outward.

Place the front side of the outer fabric with interfacing ironed on, and the front side of the lining fabric facing each other. Sew along the edges, leaving a 1 cm seam allowance. Sew three sides completely, and leave about a 10 cm opening on one side for turning. Be sure to reinforce the start and end of the seams with backstitching. If you don't have a sewing machine, you can hand sew it instead. The pure white lining fabric has no front or back side, so the creator can decide which side to use based on their preference.

Turn the book cover to the right side through the turning hole. For instructions on how to handle the corners, refer to Step 17 on page 128.

Sew the turning hole closed. Use a yellow thread that matches the fabric to sew. Refer to Step 13 on page 120 for the detailed sewing method.

Fold both the left and right sides of the book cover inward by 10 cm. The red lines in the diagram indicate the overlapping areas that need to be sewn, using the same method as in Step 10. This completes the book cover.

Tips

The wax resist dyeing process, compared to tie dye, is more suitable for expressing figurative patterns. In addition to the wax knife and wax pot, a hog bristle brush can also be used for drawing with wax, creating a textured brushstroke effect.

There are two methods for de-waxing. Besides the high-temperature ironing method introduced in this project, fabric can also be placed in water at about 60°C, where the wax will melt and float to the surface, thus de-waxing the fabric. This method is only suitable for plant dyes with high color fastness, such as indigo, as most plant dyes will re-dissolve in the water due to the high temperature, causing the fabric color to fade.

Creators may also try combining tie dye and wax resist dye, starting with folding the fabric in a regular pattern and then applying wax to resist dye. When using multiple colors in wax resist dyeing, it is important to clarify the sequence of waxing and dyeing, following the principle of working from light to dark.

中国
传统色
故宫里的色彩美学

6. Dress: *Flowing Rhythm*

This project is inspired by the natural textures of water patterns and mineral rocks. Using multi-color plant dyeing on fabric, it presents an effect where red, blue, purple, and white colors blend together.

The dress gradually transitions from cool tones at the top to warm tones at the bottom, with the hem of the dress featuring an interwoven pastel blue and pink watercolor like gradient. The use of white space in certain areas breaks the stillness of the large expanse of cool colors, creating a sense of translucence.

In the pattern design, the resist dye technique resembling marble textures creates a pattern that resembles the diffusion of water flow, as if fragmented light spots are refracted through the surface of the water. This enhances the visual depth. The irregular marks left by the thread binding resist dyeing resemble the veins of mineral rocks, subtly emerging over time, silently weaving a captivating color poem.

Material Preparation

1. Pure cotton dress, other materials are also acceptable.
2. Elastic bands, cotton cords for binding.
3. Sappanwood and alum mordant, indigo mud and alkaline agents, reducing agents.
4. Auxiliary tools: Scissors, iron, etc.

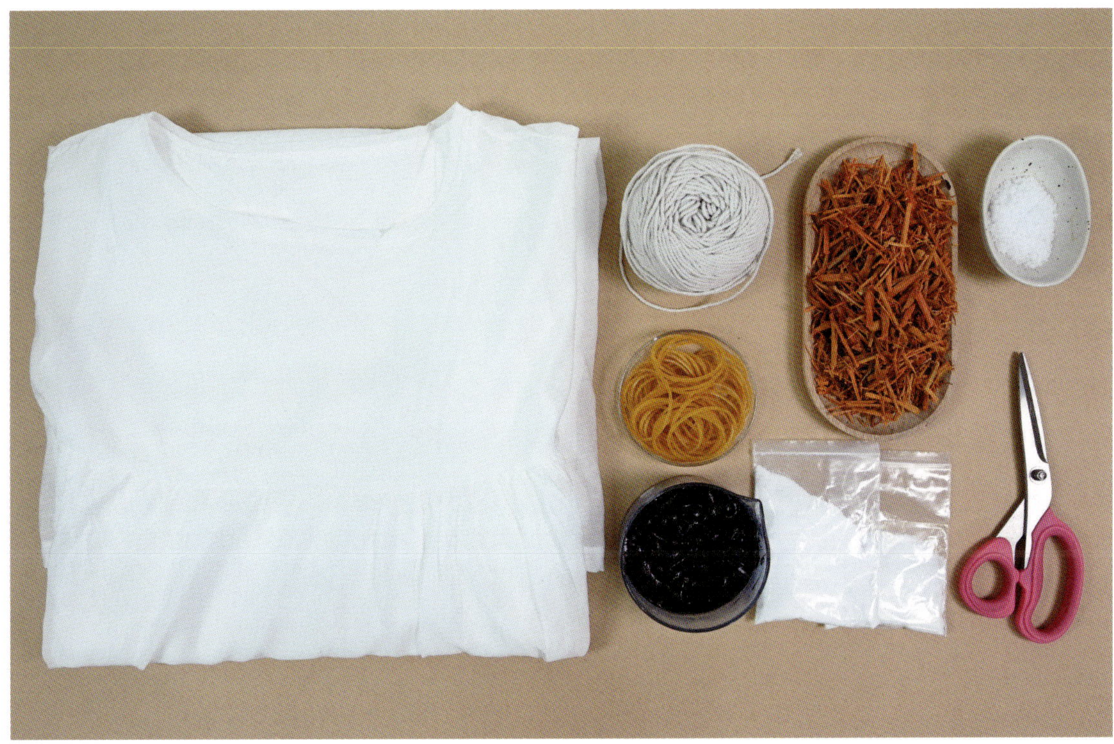

Steps

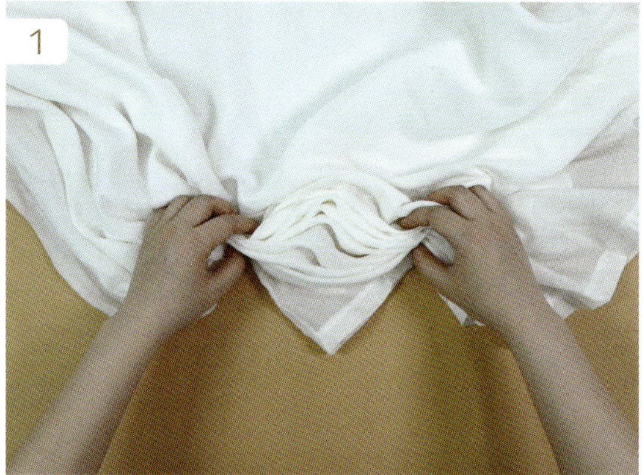

Take about a 20 × 20 cm section of fabric from the lower left corner of the front and back pieces of the dress, and fold it in a fan shape.

Compress the folded fabric into a long strip and gather it towards the center of the fold to form a bundle for tying.

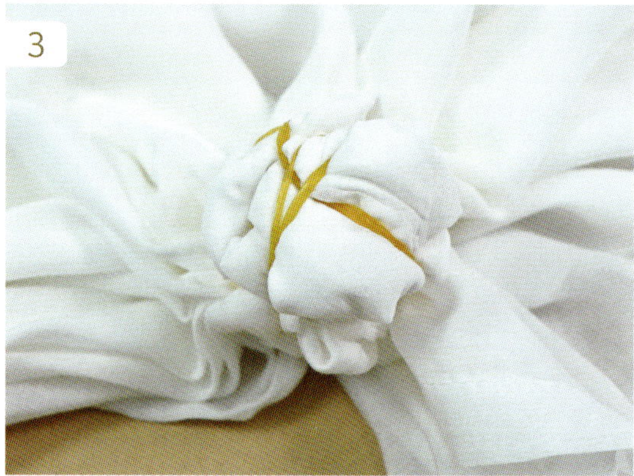

Secure the gathered fabric from Step 2 by tying it with an elastic band. This step serves to simply hold the fabric in place, and the direction or angle of the tying is not specific. It can be done randomly.

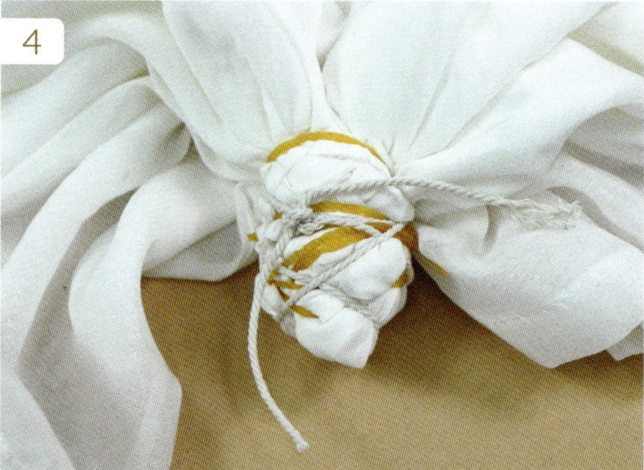

Use cotton cord to tie the fabric again. When tying, wrap the cord at multiple angles, making sure to tighten the cord with each wrap to achieve the resist dyeing effect.

Take the fabric from the upper right section of the dress and repeat Steps 1 through 4 to create and tie a second fabric bundle.

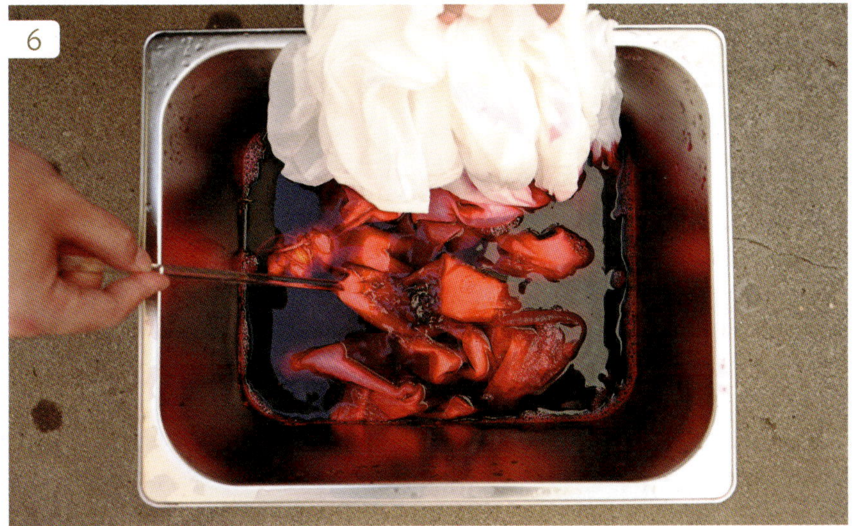

Prepare 1 L of dye solution by extracting 50 g of sappanwood, then add 4 L of clean water. As shown in the illustration, wet the dress thoroughly, then immerse only the tied sections into the dye bath, keeping the rest of the fabric out of the solution.

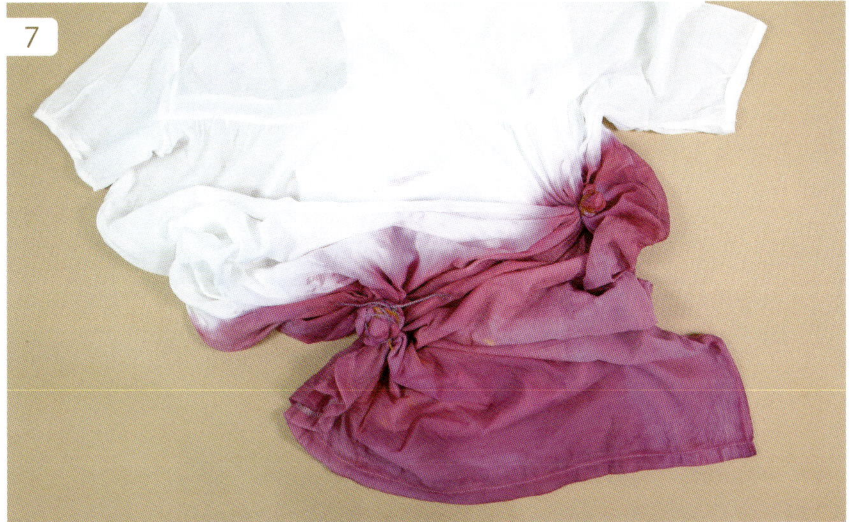

Soak the tied areas in the dye bath for 5 to 20 minutes depending on the desired depth of red. The longer the soak, the deeper the color. For this project, the fabric was dyed for 5 minutes. After dyeing, do not remove the rubber bands or cotton cord. Rinse the dress in clean water to remove excess dye and let it dry.

Lay the dress flat on the work surface, then randomly scrunch and press the fabric along the previously tie dyed areas.

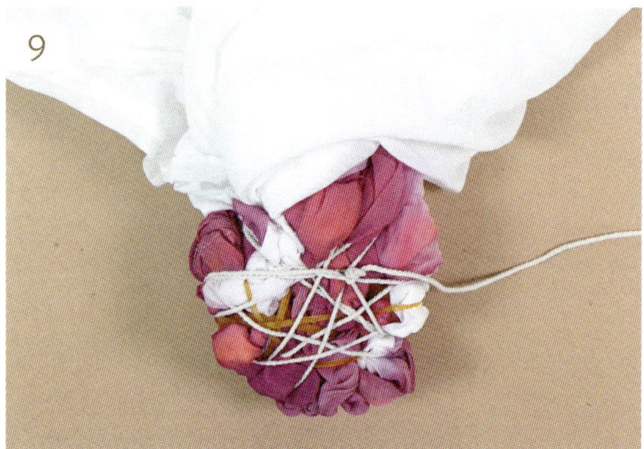

Except for the cuffs and neckline, repeat Steps 3 and 4 for the remaining parts of the dress, first securing loosely with rubber bands, then wrapping again with cotton cords. Take care to wind the cotton cord irregularly, and avoid over wrapping to prevent excessive resist dyed areas.

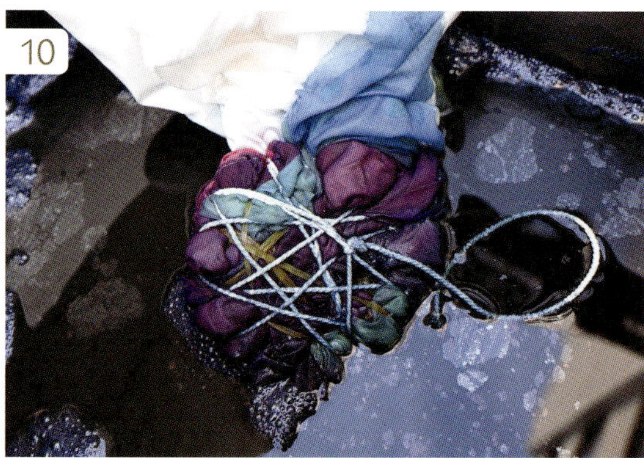

Take 30 g of indigo dye and mix it with an alkali agent and a reducing agent to prepare 300 ml of dye solution. Then dilute it with 5 L of water for dyeing. During the dyeing process, only immerse the tied sections of the fabric into the dye bath, keeping the untied parts suspended outside the liquid. It is normal for a small amount of dye to seep into the untied areas during this process.

After soaking for 5 minutes, remove the fabric and let it rest. The dyed sections will oxidize and turn from green to blue.

Tips

This project uses a marble-pattern tie dye technique for resist dyeing. As the name suggests, the resist effect resembles the crackled veins found in marble. This method allows for a high degree of creative freedom. The patterns vary depending on how the fabric is kneaded and manipulated during the binding process. The size and location of the resist areas can be adjusted according to the creator's preferences. Additionally, this project employs a dual-color dyeing process, resulting in an interplay of white, red, blue, and purple tones. In actual practice, it is also possible to dye blue first and then red.

Remove the rubber bands and cotton cords used for binding, rinse the fabric thoroughly to wash away any excess dye, then hang it to dry. The piece is now complete.

7. Cushion: *Geometry on the Tip of the Needle*

This project uses stitching as a resist technique to prevent dye penetration. The stitching lines are pulled tight to block the dye, and the different sewing paths, along with sewing through multiple folded layers of fabric, create rich and intricate patterns. The writer has carefully designed various stitching techniques, combining sewing with dyeing to produce unique and complex designs.

The cushion is based on simple square and circular geometric shapes, dividing the surface into different striped or ring like sections. These are stitched using dashed lines, zigzags, and intersecting lines, creating a rich sense of depth and texture. The deep blue background contrasts sharply with the white patterns formed by the resist dyeing, adding warmth and tranquility to the home decor.

Material Preparation

1. White cotton or plain fabric: 4 pieces of the front fabric, each measuring 50 × 50 cm; 8 pieces of backing fabric, each measuring 35 × 50 cm.
2. Hand sewing cotton thread, specification: 4 ply thread.
3. Indigo dye.
4. Auxiliary tools: Sewing needles, water soluble pen, fabric ruler, compass, scissors, etc.

Operating Tips

This set of projects will be explained in two parts: the first part focuses on tie dye and sewing operations, while the second part covers the dyeing and cushion-making process. The tie dye and sewing operations will vary slightly for the four cushions, which are explained as Cushion A, B, C, and D. The dyeing and cushion-making process will be explained using a single example for all.

In the tie dye and sewing operations, the steps will be explained using both demonstration images and schematic diagrams. The schematic diagrams are standard, to scale, and should be used as a reference for drawing and sewing. For ease of viewing, the demonstration piece alternates between red and blue cotton threads, but readers are encouraged to use white cotton thread for actual practice. In the schematic diagrams, the red and blue threads correspond to those in the demonstration piece, with the light red and light blue stitches representing the hand sewn stitches on the fabric's reverse side. All measurements are in centimeters.

❖Cushion A

On the white cotton fabric, use a water soluble pen to draw a square with a side length of 12 cm, centered as shown in the schematic diagram. Then, divide the square into reference lines with a 0.7 cm spacing, as indicated in the diagram.

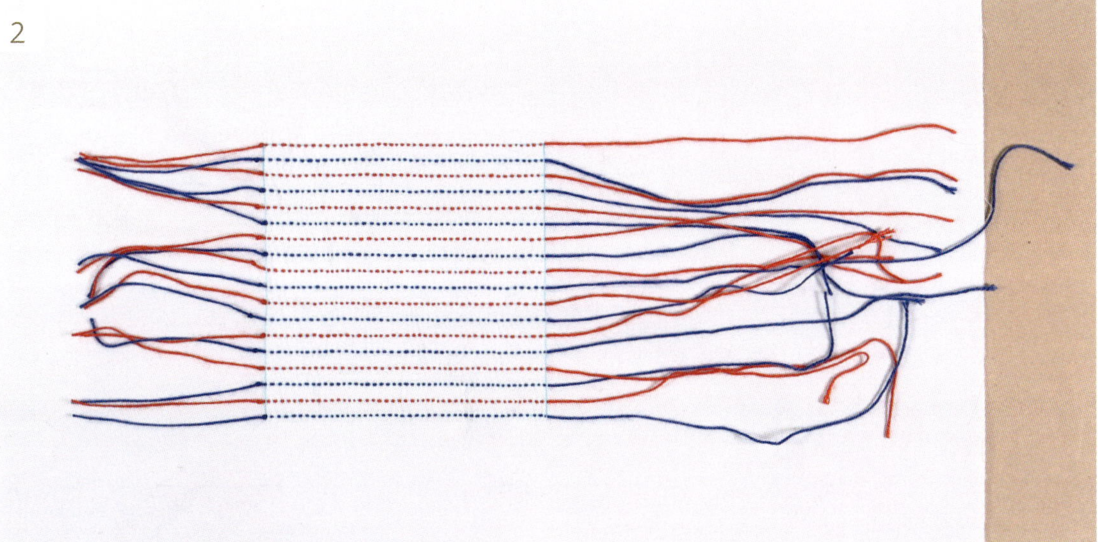

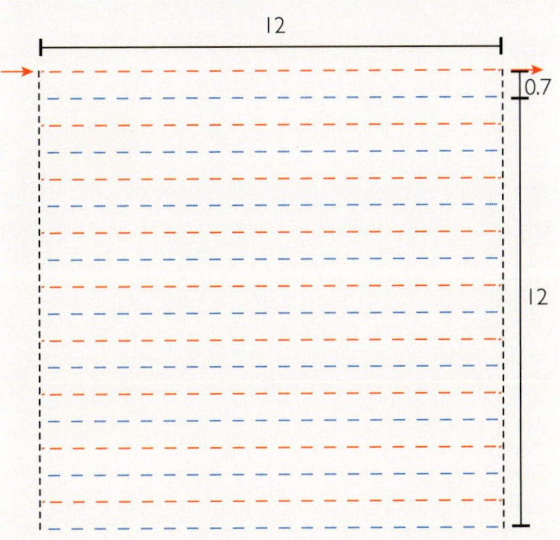

Hand sew along the reference lines on the white cotton fabric. Tie a knot at one end of the thread, making sure to tie it 3 to 4 times to ensure the knot doesn't pull through the fabric when tightening the thread later. Sew along each reference line as shown in the diagram on the left, leaving about 10 cm of excess thread at the end before cutting it. It is important to make sure that the red and blue dashed lines alternate as much as possible while sewing, as this will make the final pattern after dyeing more aesthetically pleasing. Stitch 10 to 14 stitches per 3 cm.

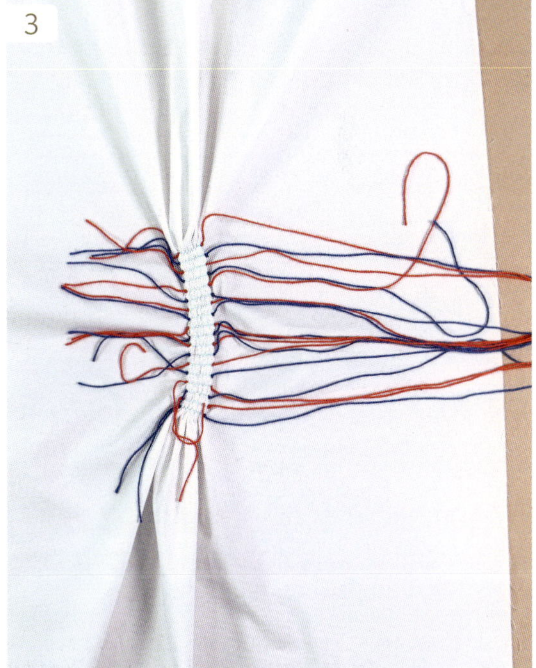

Tighten the thread at the ends of the lines, tying a knot at each one. The tighter the thread is pulled, the clearer the pattern will be after dyeing.

Tips

Hold the end knot with one hand and use the other hand to firmly squeeze the tightened fabric. If there are gaps in the cotton thread at the knot, it indicates that the thread hasn't been completely tightened. Continue tying knots and move the new knot position towards the thread. Repeat the process several times until the knot is fully tightened.

❖Cushion B

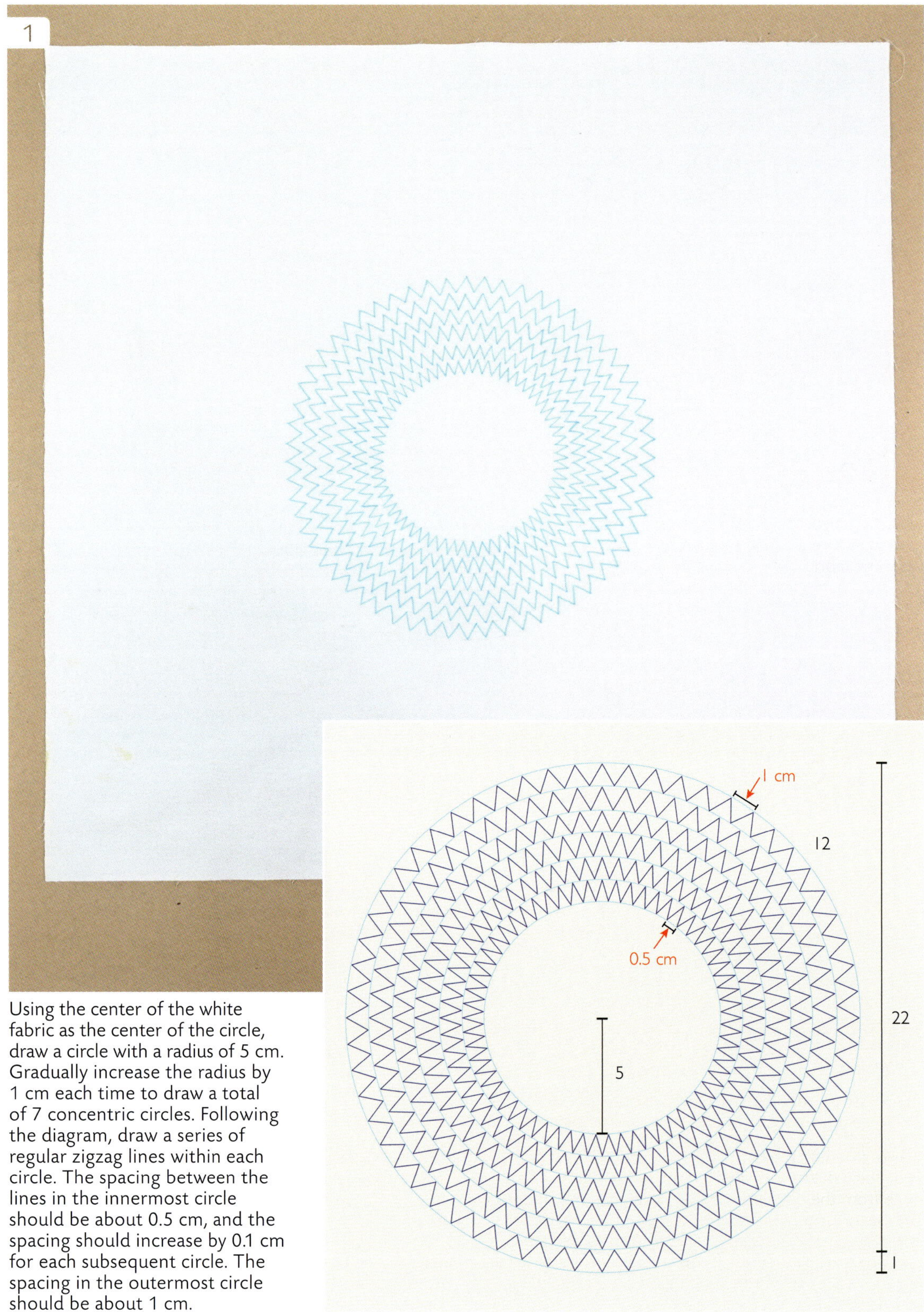

Using the center of the white fabric as the center of the circle, draw a circle with a radius of 5 cm. Gradually increase the radius by 1 cm each time to draw a total of 7 concentric circles. Following the diagram, draw a series of regular zigzag lines within each circle. The spacing between the lines in the innermost circle should be about 0.5 cm, and the spacing should increase by 0.1 cm for each subsequent circle. The spacing in the outermost circle should be about 1 cm.

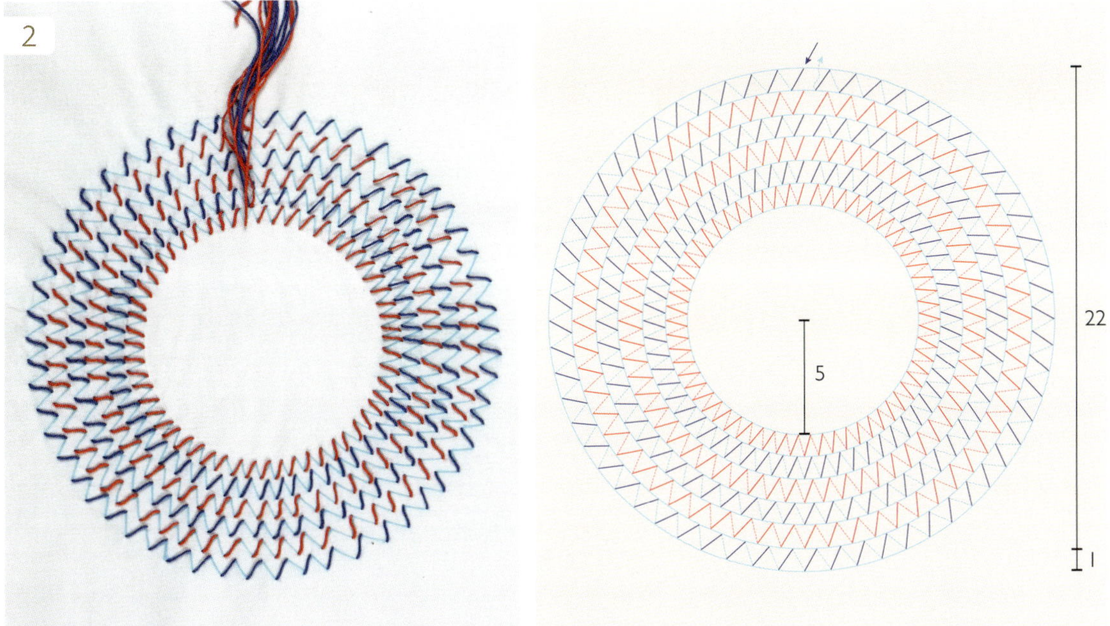

Choose any point within the circle as the starting point, and sew along the circular path with the zigzag lines as the stitch distance. Leave about 10 cm of excess thread at the end and cut it off. Repeat this process for each circle. Be sure to ensure that the start and end points of the six circular rings remain on the same horizontal line. When sewing, keep the fabric flat and avoid puckering.

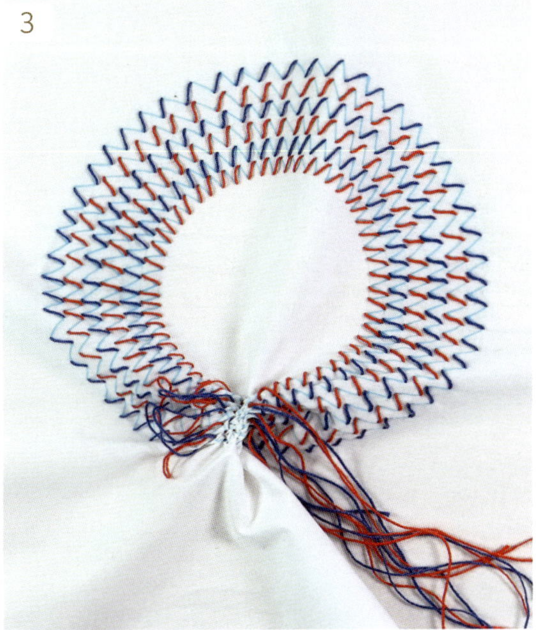

Start tightening the fabric from the thread knot at one end. Since the folded lines cannot be tightened all at once from the end, it should be done gradually in small amounts. It is recommended to tighten 2 to 4 sections at a time, and all 6 circles of folded lines should be tightened simultaneously. Otherwise, it will cause local fabric wrinkles to accumulate, making the remaining sewing folds difficult to distinguish.

Once all 6 circles of folded lines are tightened, tie knots one by one.

❖Cushion C

Center a square with a side length of 20 cm on the white cotton fabric and draw horizontal reference lines according to the spacing values shown in the schematic diagram.

Draw the reference lines according to the blue shapes shown in the schematic diagram.

Sew according to the schematic diagram below. For straight stitching, refer to Cushion A. For zigzag stitching, refer to Cushion B. For cross stitching, follow the order indicated by the left arrows in the schematic diagram. Solid lines represent the stitching on the front side, while dotted lines represent the stitching on the back side. The gray blocks in the schematic diagram indicate fabric folds. Light gray represents a fabric folded in half, and medium gray represents a fan shaped fold with three layers. When sewing, you can first fold the fabric to create crease lines and secure with pins or clips.

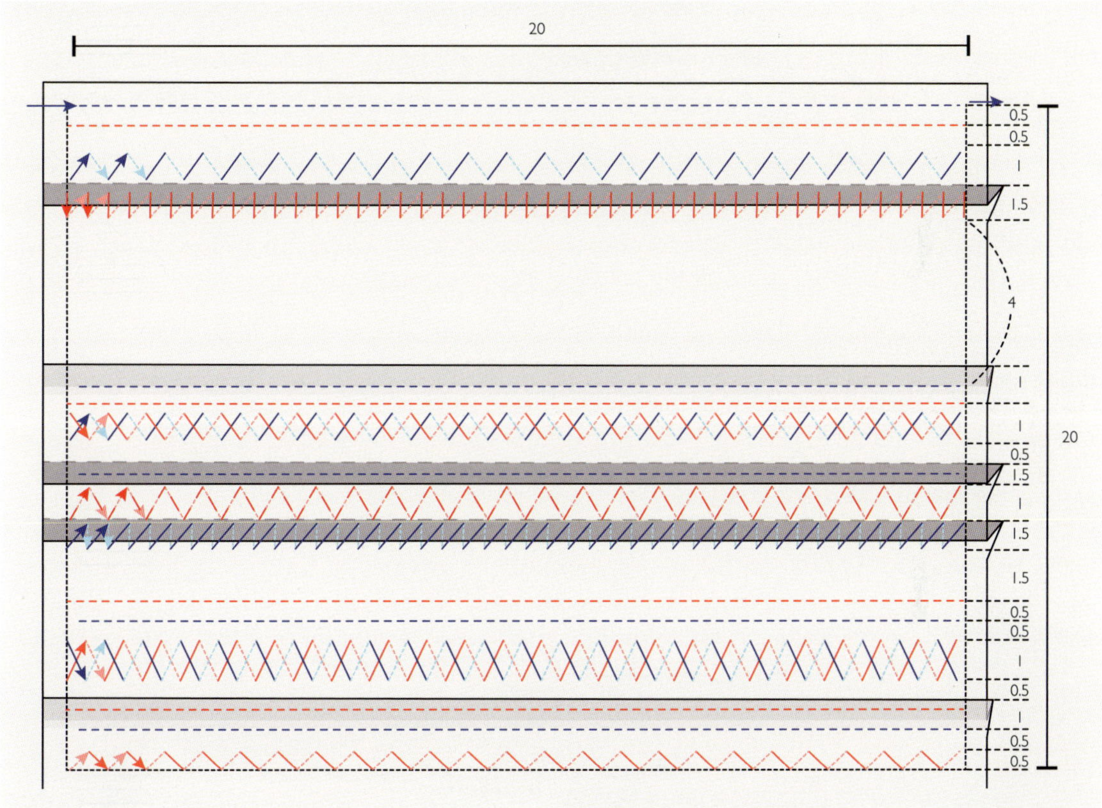

20

0.5
0.5
1
1.5
4
1
1
0.5
1.5
1
1.5
1.5
0.5
0.5
1
0.5
1
0.5
0.5

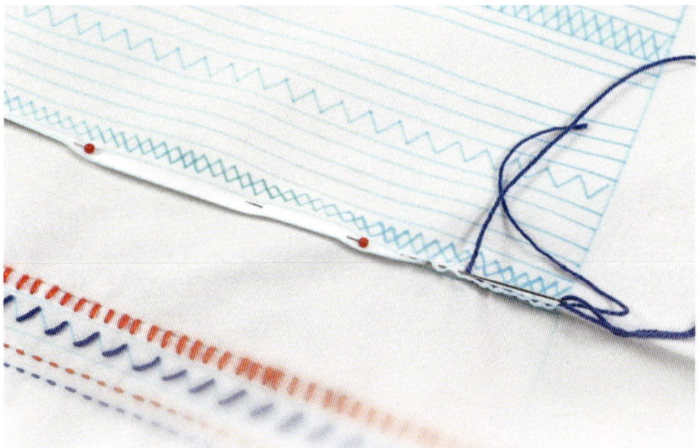

20

Detailed reference diagram for half fold

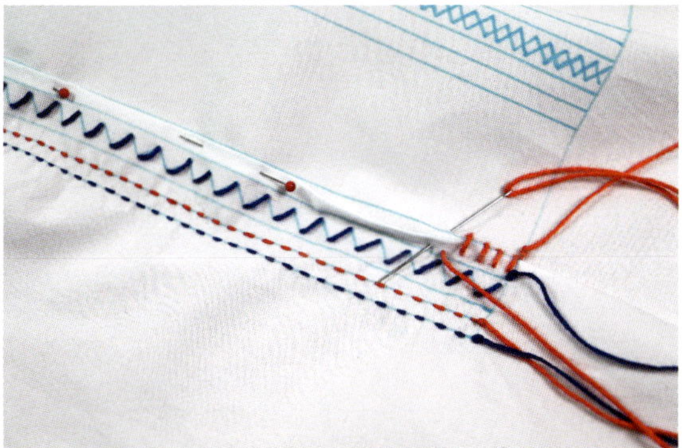

Detailed reference diagram for trifold

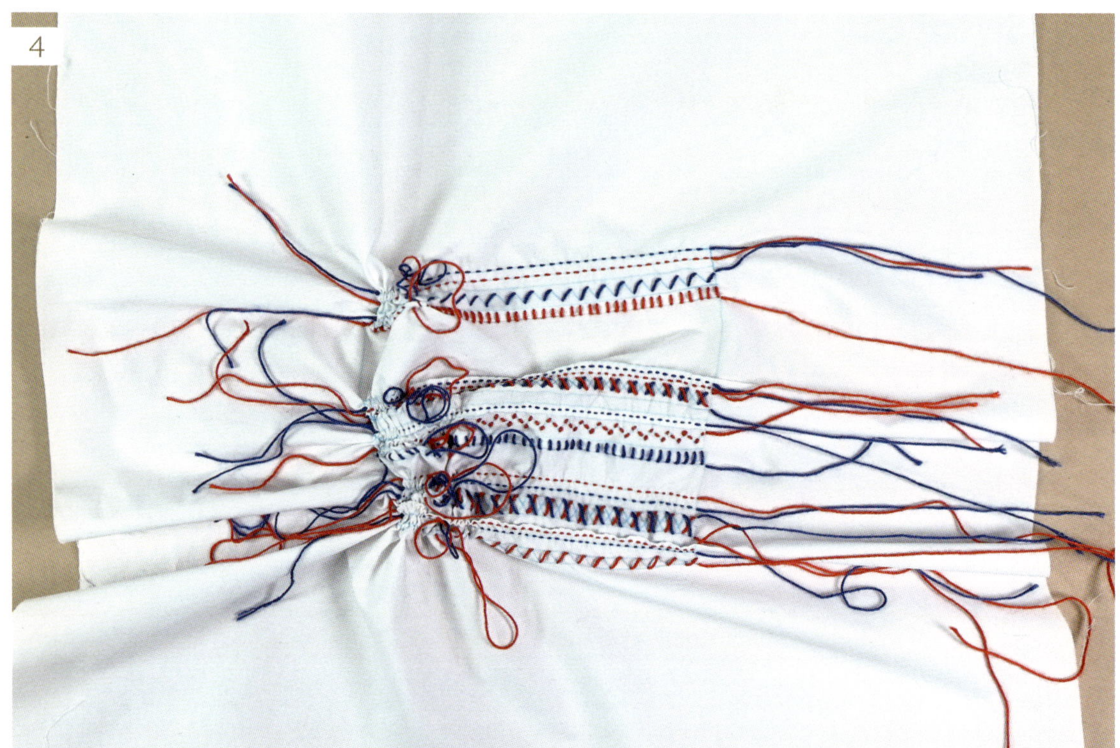

Tighten the fabric along the end of the thread, pulling in small amounts and gradually tightening each section, 2 to 4 segments at a time. During this process, you may use tools such as a needle or awl to help pull and tighten the threads. All the segments must be tightened simultaneously.

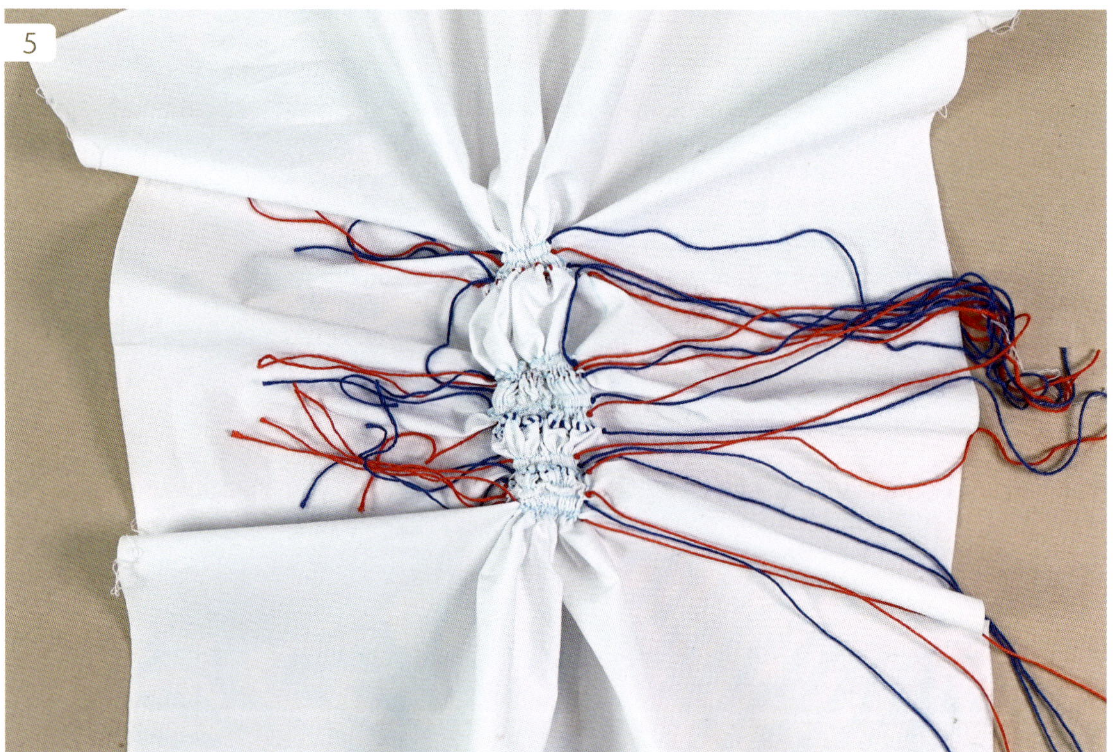

Once all the segments are tightened, tie knots in sequence.

❖Cushion D

On the white cotton fabric, draw a diamond shape centered with a side length of 20 cm. Then, draw horizontal reference lines based on the spacing values shown in the schematic diagram. The image on the left shows the effect from a 45-degree rotated perspective to the left.

Draw the reference lines according to the blue shapes shown in the schematic diagram.

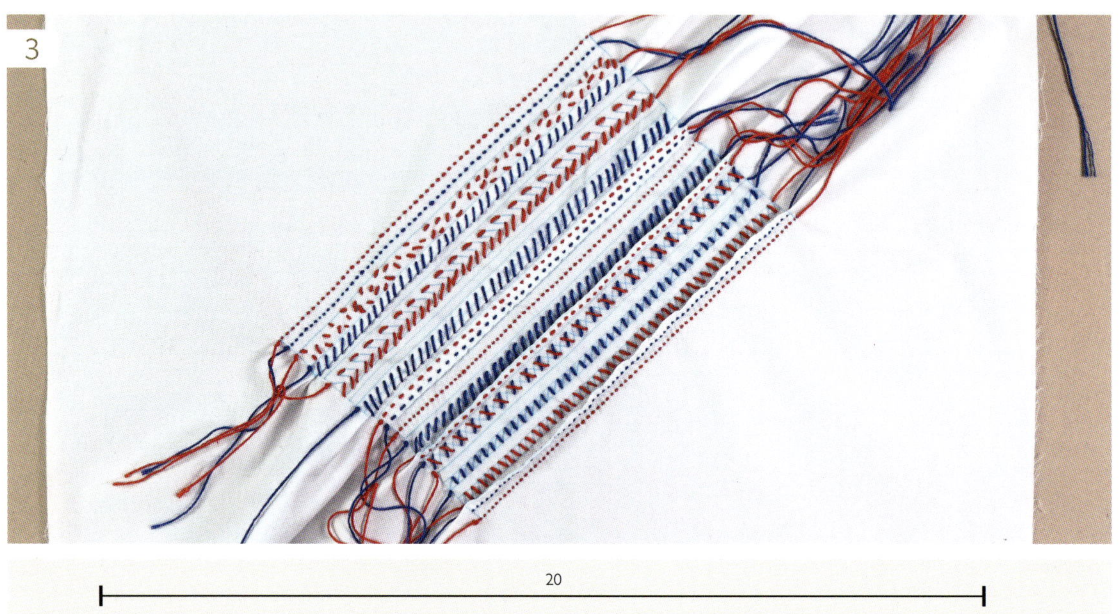

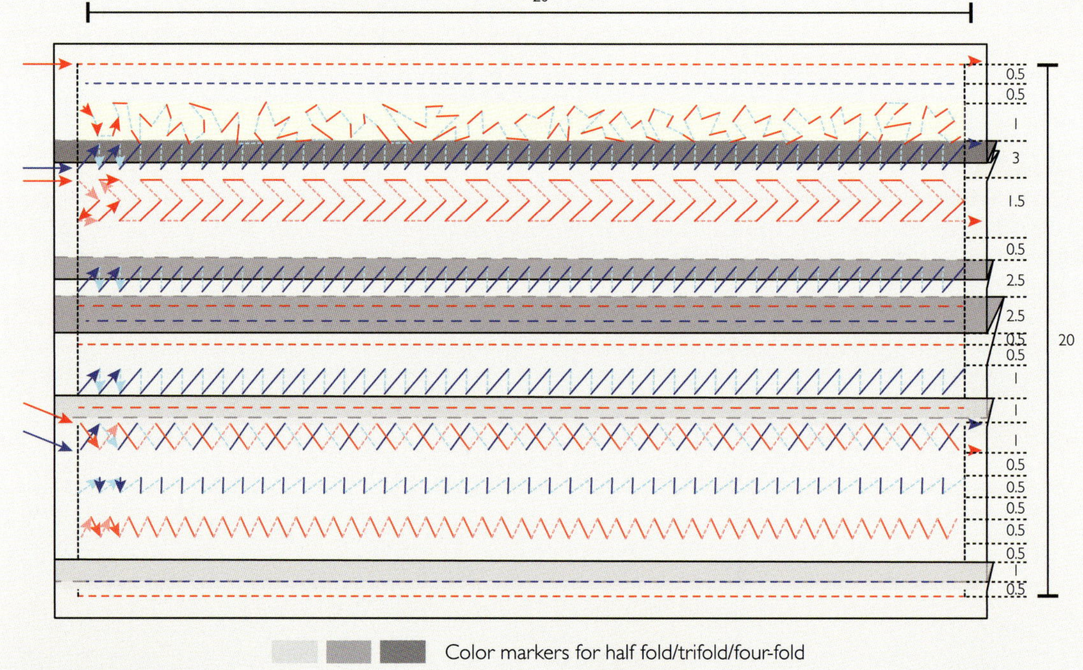

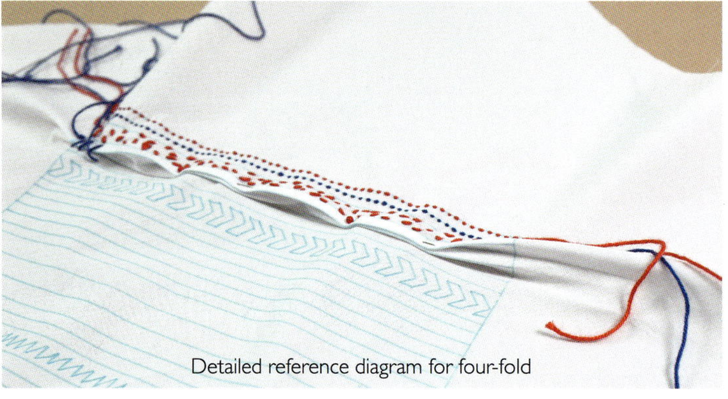
Detailed reference diagram for four-fold

Sew according to the schematic diagram. For straight line sewing, refer to Cushion A. For zigzag sewing, refer to Cushion B, and for crisscross line sewing, refer to Cushion C. The gray areas in the diagram indicate fabric folding, divided into three types: light gray represents a simple fold to form two layers, medium gray represents a fan fold with three layers, and dark gray represents a fan fold with four layers. The yellow area in the diagram shows free stitching, where short stitches are used with random stitch direction. The sewing is done from one side to the other.

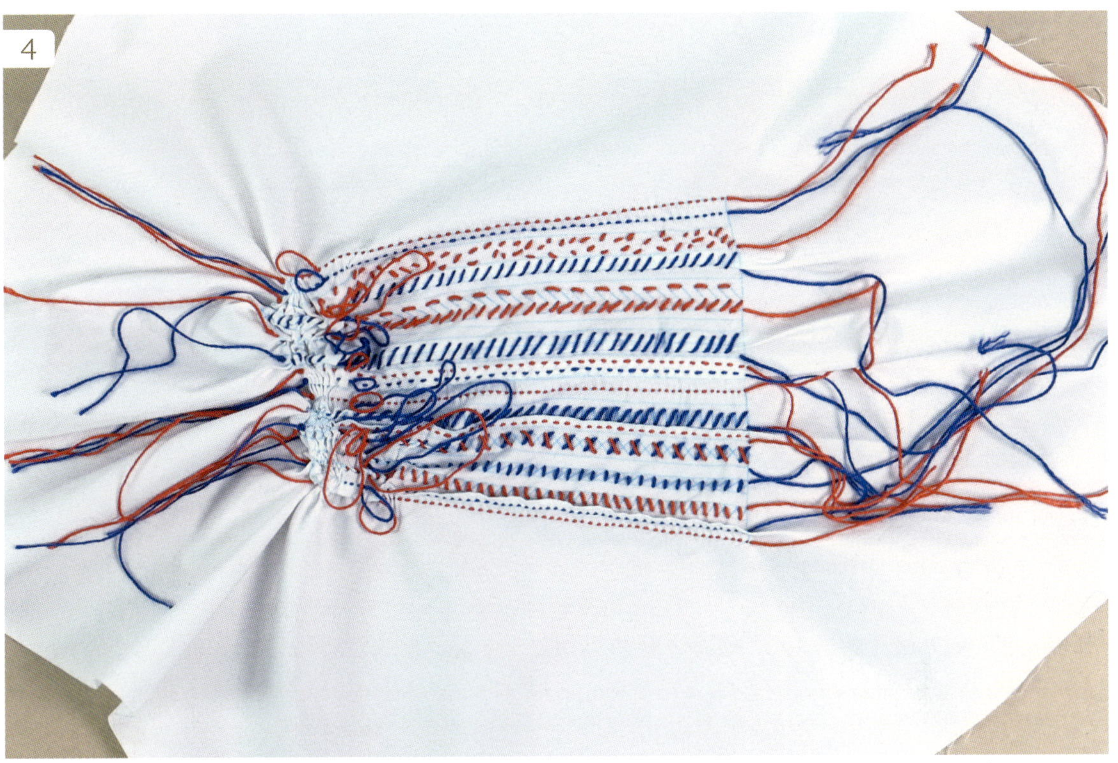

Tighten the fabric along the end of the thread knot. It should be done gradually and in small sections, tightening 2 to 4 segments at a time. During this process, you can use tools such as a needle or awl to help pull the threads tight. All segments must be tightened simultaneously.

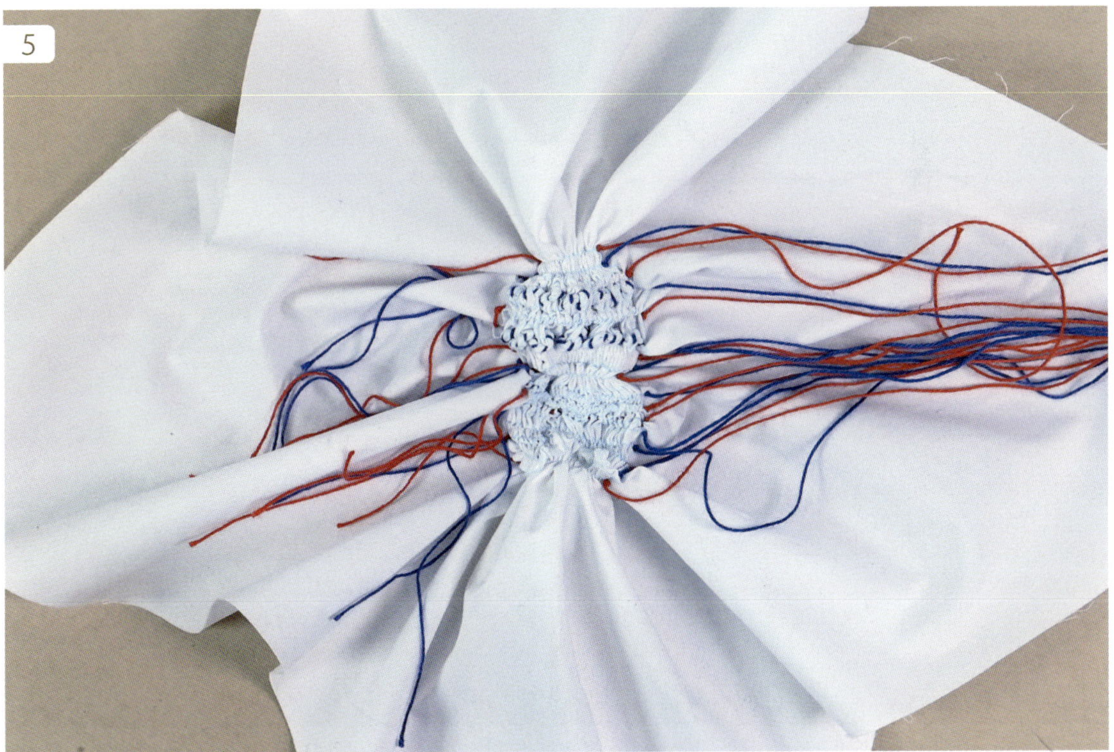

Once all segments are tightened, tie knots in sequence.

❖Dyeing and Cushion Making

Prepare 400 to 500 g of indigo paste, mix with alkali, reducing agent, and water to make 4,000 to 5,000 ml of dye liquid. For specific instructions, refer to the section on Indigo Dye Extraction on page 65–68. To ensure even and thorough dyeing, it is recommended to handle each piece individually. Before dyeing, moisten the fabric and immerse it in the dye. The depth of the color can be adjusted according to personal preference, with the four cushions in this project being dyed 3, 5, 6, and 6 times, respectively. The backing fabric is also dyed using this step.

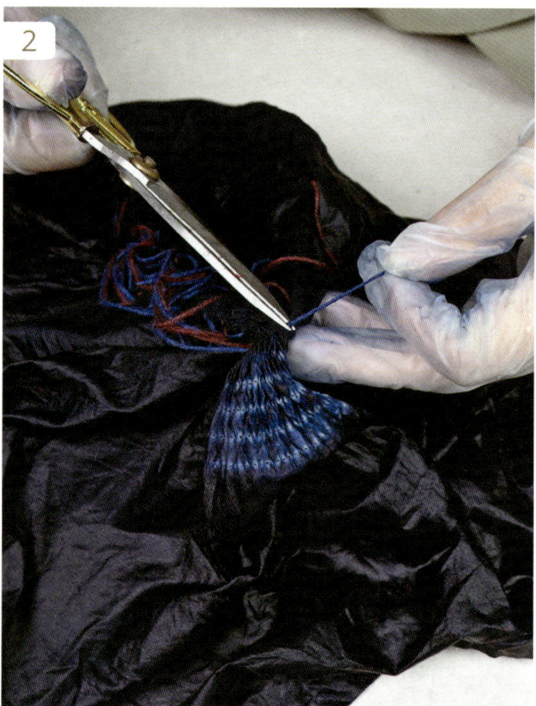

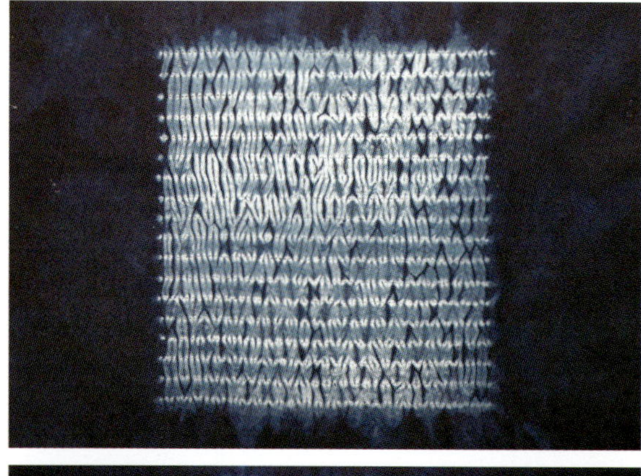

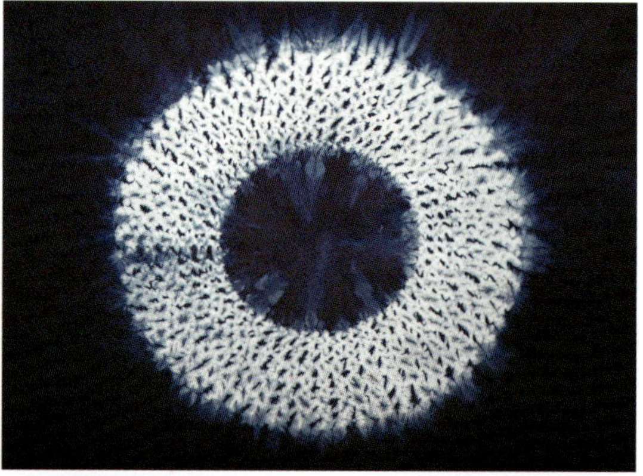

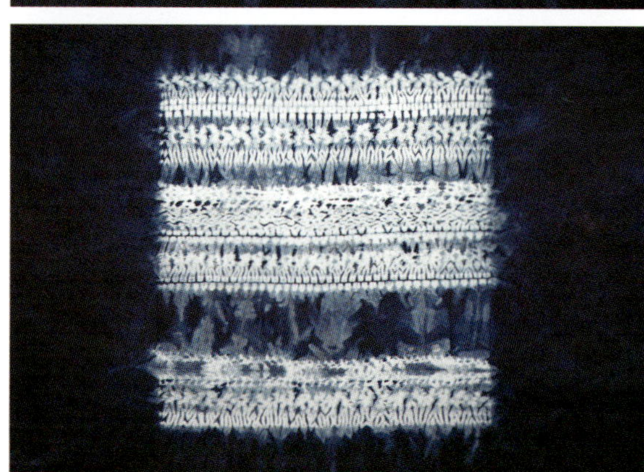

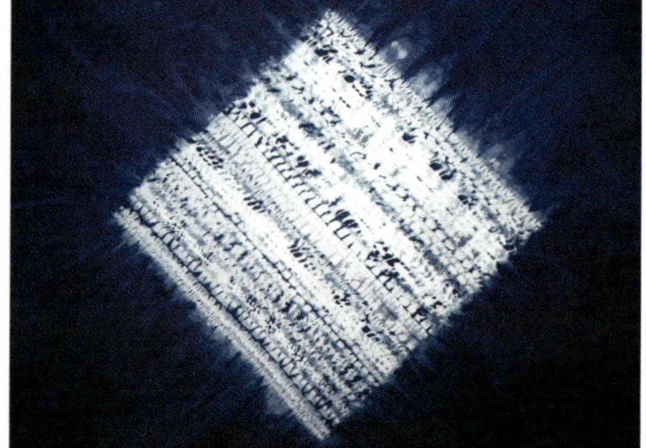

After dyeing, briefly wash the fabric to remove excess color. Remove the sewing thread and carefully wash the fabric to ensure all excess color is thoroughly cleaned.

Cut the front fabric and back fabric. The original size of the front fabric is 50 × 50 cm. Center the pattern and cut it to 47 × 47 cm. The original size of the back fabric is 35 × 50 cm. Cut it to 32 × 47 cm, and cut 2 pieces. Since the back fabric does not have a tie dye pattern, dampen the back fabric, lightly scrunch it, and then dip it into the dye bath. This will create a fabric with a soft, gradient texture, as shown in the picture. This step can be done based on personal preference.

Take one piece of the back fabric and fold one long edge inward twice, each fold 0.5 cm wide, and sew along this edge. Both hand stitching and machine stitching are acceptable. This step will hide the fabric's raw edges. Perform the same operation on the other piece of back fabric.

5

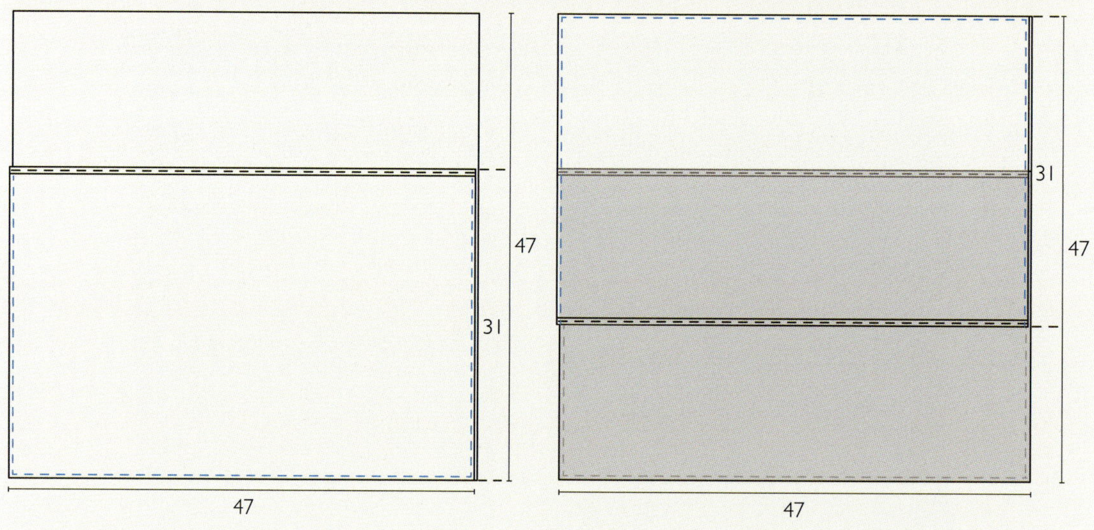

When hand dyeing the fabric, the degree of contact between the front and back fabric and the dye solution may cause slight differences in the pattern. You can distinguish the front and back of the fabric based on personal preference. Once the front and back sides of the front and back fabric have been identified, place the front fabric with one piece of back fabric, with the wrong sides facing each other. Align the long edge of the back fabric that has not undergone Step 4 with any side of the front fabric, and sew 0.5 cm from the edge of the fabric. Perform the same operation with the other piece of back fabric. There will be a 15 cm overlap between the two pieces of back fabric. Sew all three layers of fabric together in the overlapping area. The two edges that were folded will now be in the middle section of the cushion, forming an opening. After the production is completed, the cushion insert can be placed through this opening.

Turn the fabric from the opening so that the back side is facing out, with the front sides of the fabric facing each other. When flipping the fabric, fold the corners according to the method described in Step 17 on page 128. Tidy up the seam allowance along the fabric edge and press it flat with an iron. Then sew around the edge at 0.5 cm from the edge.

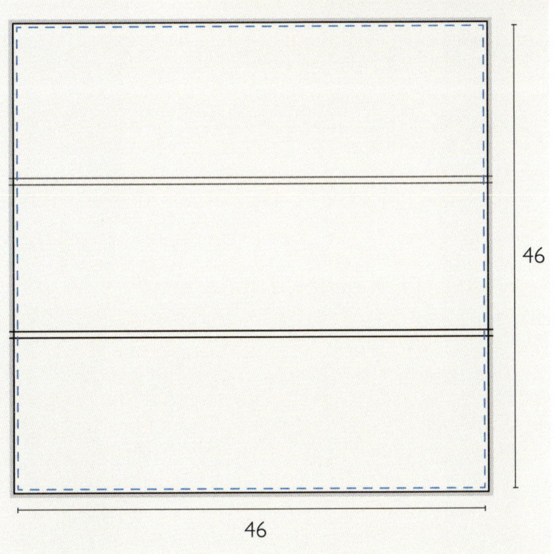

Turn the fabric right side out through the opening. Iron the seam allowance at the fabric edge to smooth it out. Place the cushion insert into the pillowcase, and the cushion making is now complete.

Tips

This project is divided into two parts. The first part involves using sewing techniques for resist dyeing, and the second part covers dyeing and cushion making. Readers can personalize their designs by using the resist dyeing sewing technique combined with various sewing methods and stitch techniques to create countless pattern effects. The outer contours can go beyond geometric shapes, and the size can be adjusted according to personal preferences. You can even use fabric design to create not just cushions but other home décor products as well.

8. Curtain: *Landscape of Lakes and Mountains*

This project takes traditional Chinese landscape painting as its creative inspiration, rendered in a dominant bright yellow tone and expressed through a combination of tie dye and embroidery techniques.

The tie dye sections use resist dyeing through binding to create alternating yellow and white ripple patterns, evoking the shimmering surface of a lake. Within this wave like background, motifs of water patterns and bridges are embroidered. Embroidery is also used to depict a continuous range of mountains, outlining the undulating contours and layered silhouettes to convey the grandeur and majesty of rivers and mountains. Meanwhile, the winding waterway flowing alongside the mountains and the scattered trees dotting the slopes add a sense of tranquility and depth, evoking the refined essence of China's natural scenery and a mindset of peaceful detachment.

Material Preparation

1. White linen: 2 pieces, each measuring 200 × 50 cm. This piece uses relatively stiff linen with high light transmittance.
2. Two design templates, each measuring 50 × 180 cm(templates can be found on page 168. Creators may choose whether to add embroidery based on personal preference).
3. Thread for binding, and white cotton embroidery thread.
4. Dye plants: 150 g of gardenia fruit and 50 g of sappanwood.
5. Mordant: Ferrous sulphate.
6. Auxiliary tools: Heat erasable pen, hand sewing needles, scissors, ruler, iron, etc.

Steps

1

Print the full size design templates and place them centered beneath the linen fabric. Using a heat erasable pen, trace the horizontal dividing lines from the template onto the linen. These marked areas represent the water ripples and bridge sections in the design and will be processed with tie dye. There is one such area near the bottom of the left panel, and two near the bottom of the right panel.

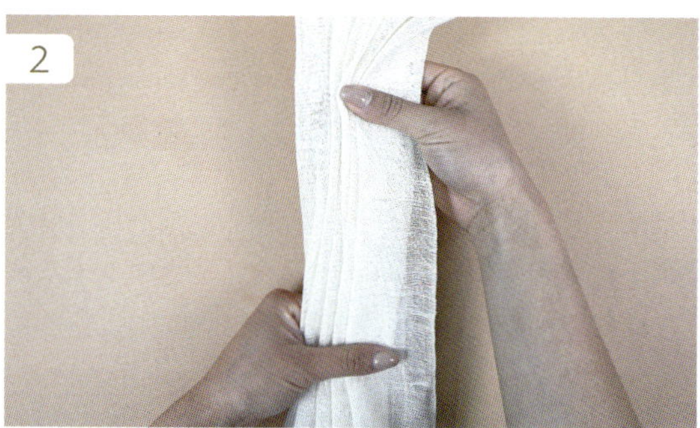

2

Take either panel and fold the area to be tie dyed into a fan shape, with each fold approximately 4 cm wide.

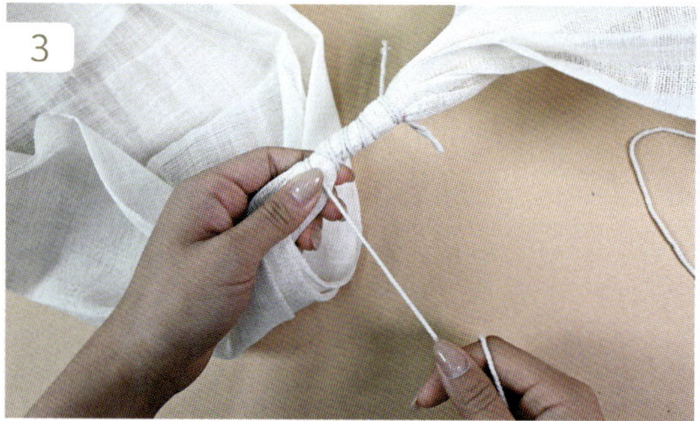

3

Use cotton cord to bind the fabric. Start by wrapping the cord 3 to 4 times around one marked point and tie a knot. Then continue wrapping toward the opposite marked point. Be sure to pull the cord tight before each successive wrap to ensure a clear resist dye pattern. While wrapping, vary the spacing between the cords to create a visually interesting binding effect with alternating widths.

4

After wrapping to the opposite marked point, secure the end by wrapping the cord 3 to 4 times and tying a knot, then cut off the excess cord. The completed binding effect for both the left and right curtain panels should appear as shown in the image.

5

Extract 5 L of dye solution with 250 g of gardenia, then add an additional 3 L of clean water. Pour the mixture into an open container with a capacity of over 8 L. Soak the two curtain panels in water to dampen them, then fully immerse them in the dye bath for 1 hour. Stir the fabric continuously during this time to ensure even coloring.

6

Remove the curtain panels from the dye bath and rinse them with clean water to wash off any excess dye. Hang them to dry.

Use an iron to press and flatten the fabric. As shown in the image, the tie dyed areas reveal yellow and white wave patterns and crease marks formed by the folding.

Place the template underneath the linen. Pin the template and fabric together using pins. Then, use a heat erasable pen to trace the design onto the fabric.

Dye the embroidery thread by extracting 50 g of sappanwood into 1 L of dye liquid, then add 4 g of ferrous sulphate as a mordant. Wet the white cotton thread, then soak it in the dye solution for 2 hours. After dyeing, rinse the thread with water to remove excess dye and let it dry. You can also skip this step by using pre-colored embroidery thread in a suitable shade.

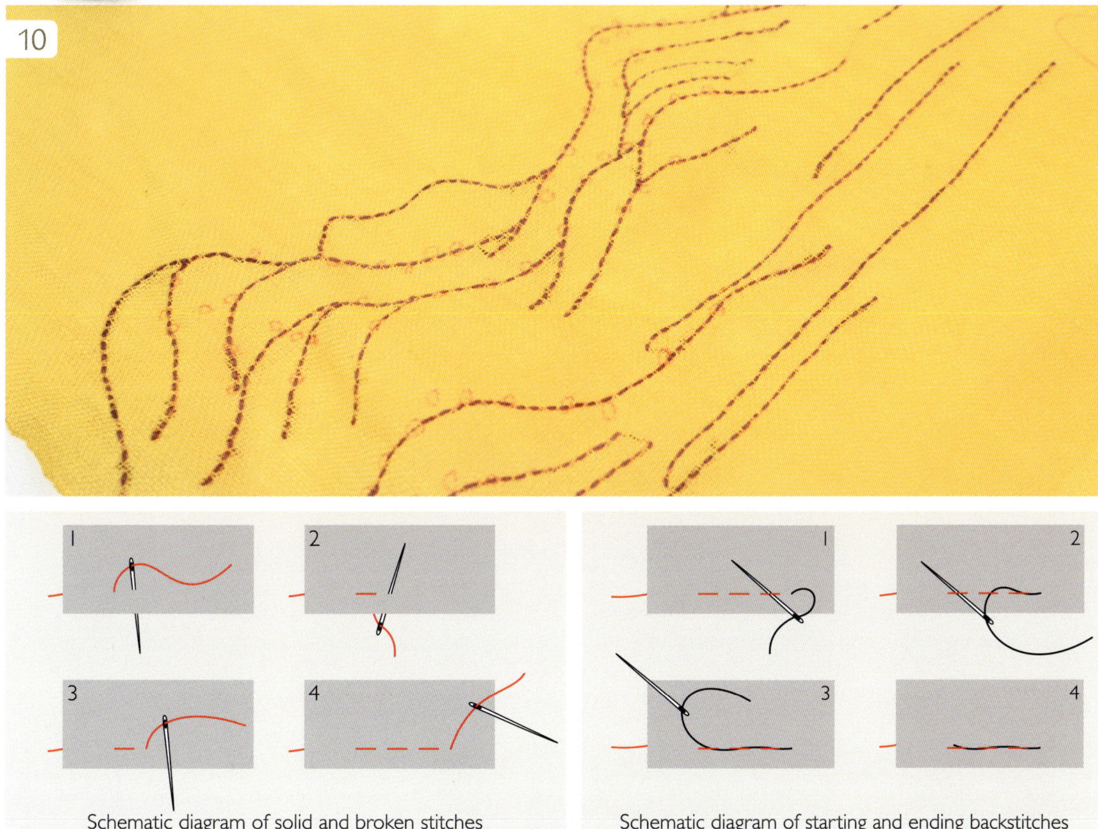

Schematic diagram of solid and broken stitches

Schematic diagram of starting and ending backstitches

All the mountain and water lines in the picture are embroidered using a combination of solid and broken stitches. When embroidering, use about 60 cm of thread each time. Avoid pulling the thread too tightly to prevent the fabric from wrinkling. Regarding the stitch crossing, if the gap between one line segment and the next is less than 1.5 cm, you can directly cross the stitches and continue embroidering. Otherwise, you need to go back and cut the thread, then re-start the stitch. If the crossing stitches are too long, it will result in a messy back and the stitches may show up on the front in areas with lighter colors.

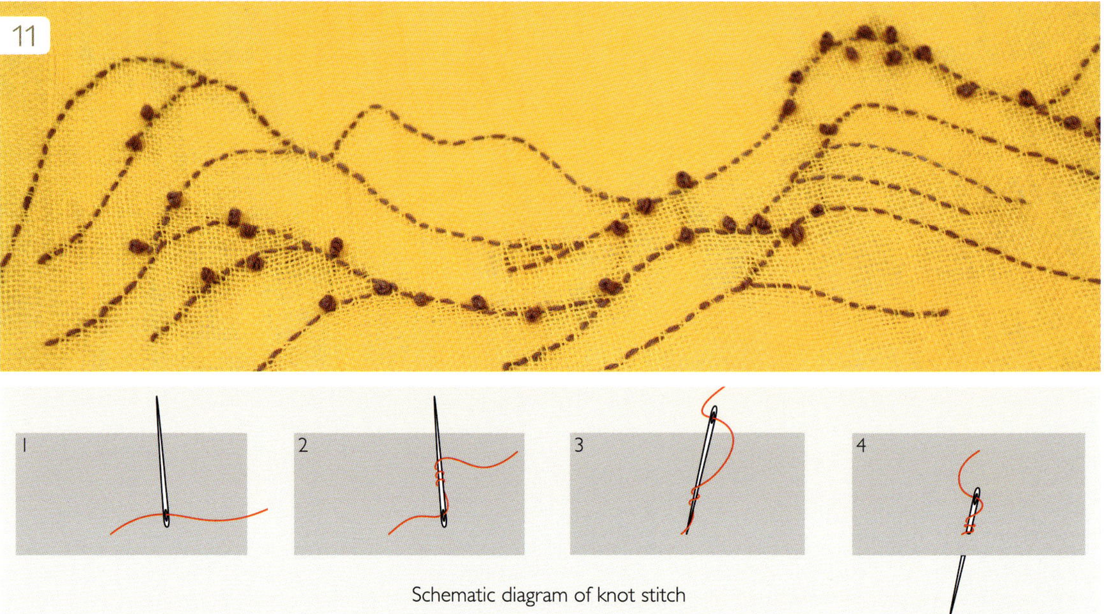

Schematic diagram of knot stitch

The small and large dots in the picture represent trees on the mountain and are embroidered using knot stitch. The number of knot stitch loops can be determined based on the size of the dots in the picture. It is recommended to vary the sizes for a more pleasing effect. The cotton thread used in this piece is approximately 0.8 mm thick, and the knot stitch loops range from 2 to 4 loops.

Iron the fabric curtain to make it smooth, then trim the edges, leaving a 5 cm seam allowance at both the top and bottom to create the rod pocket. The cutting dimensions should be 50 × 190 cm. Mark a 1 cm distance from the edge using a heat erasable pen.

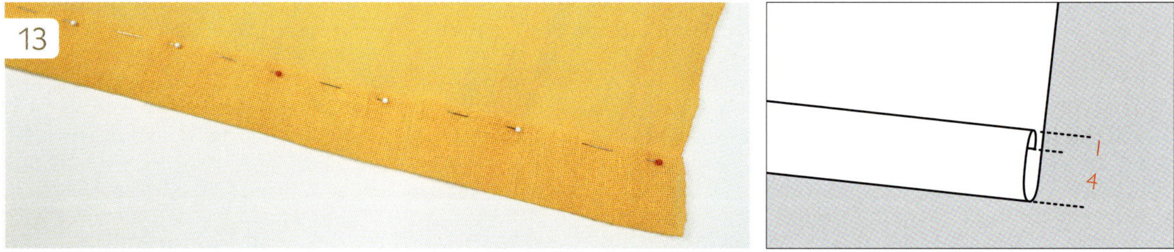

Trim any excess fabric along the edges, fold as shown in the diagram, and secure it with pins.

Use a hidden stitch to sew the top and bottom edges of the rod pocket, completing the curtain. For detailed instructions on the hidden stitch, refer to Step 13 on page 120.

Tips

This project primarily uses embroidery as the main form of expression, carrying the depiction of all the figurative content, while dyeing serves as a supporting technique to present the imagery of flowing water. This is also the highlight of the piece, as it leaves room for the viewer's imagination through this approach. During the creative process, various techniques and methods can be integrated, utilizing the strengths of each craft to express the desired content.

Templates

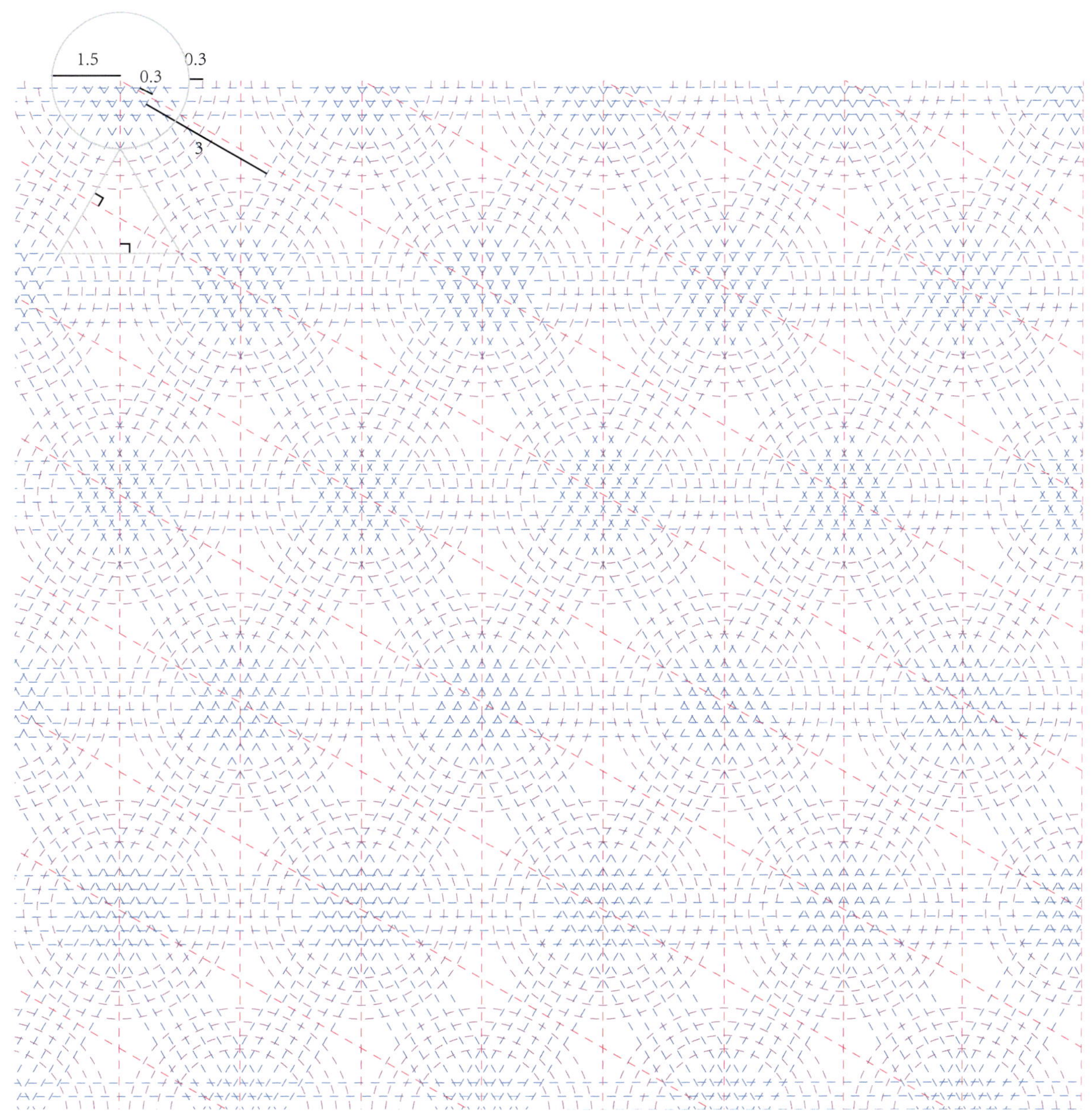

Reference line diagram for placemat—*Turtle's Blessing*.

On the facing page
A batik work featuring plant motifs, dyed with gardenia and indigo.

Complete line diagram for placemat—*Turtle's Blessing*.

Pattern for book cover—*Possessing Abundant Knowledge*.

Design templates for curtain—*Landscape of Lakes and Mountains*.